THIS BEAUTIFUL THING
CALLED CHURCH

THIS BEAUTIFUL THING CALLED CHURCH

KEITH LIVINGSTON

XULON PRESS

Xulon Press
2301 Lucien Way #415
Maitland, FL 32751
407.339.4217
www.xulonpress.com

Printed in the United States of America.

ISBN-13: 978-1-5456-7521-2

November, 2019

For Dr Pearce,
Thank you for keeping
an eye on my birthday
suit!

DEDICATION

TO THE JOY OF MY LIFE – MY WIFE KATHY

AND MY MARVELOUS FAMILY: LEE, KRIS, ANNALISE & DANIEL

STEVE, CECI & EMANUEL

ACKNOWLEDGMENTS

MY THANKS TO: CAREY & TONI, LEE & KRIS, STEVE & CECI, NANCY, CHRIS AND JOHN & DONNA

FOR THEIR TIRELESS EDITING ASSISTANCE

TABLE OF CONTENTS

Dedication.. vii
Acknowledgments.................................... ix
Foreword..xiii

1. This Beautiful Thing Called Church...................1
2. The Dusty Road 16
3. Happy Childhood 20
4. Making Molasses And Killing Hogs..................26
5. A Life Spared 32
6. A Miserable Summer............................. 38
7. Revival 41
8. School Days 45
9. Forbidden Love.................................. 49
10. East Central Junior College 62
11. A Five And Dime Career..........................66
12. Did The National Guard Save Me From Marriage?......74
13. Officer Candidate School - OCS Class R60 78
14. My Military Career...............................87
15. Meeting The One 94
16. Summer Of 61.................................. 98
17. Honeymooning In Florida – Not Really 102
18. 133 1/3 Prentiss Street...........................105

19. New Furniture, New Job,
    New Car, Night School 109
20. Hired By IBM – Wow 114
21. An IBM Manager – Wow 121
22. Baton Rouge – A Sportsman's Paradise 126
23. The Miracle 131
24. The Jackson Mississippi Years 139
25. Finally A Church Family 147
26. The Making Of A Certified Public Accountant 150
27. The Debacle Of A Second Line Manager 153
28. The New Jersey Experience 158
29. At Home In The Old Dominion 170
30. The Prison Ministry 188
31. Crosslink International 201
32. Retirement 205
33. Anniversaries 209
34. A Prayer Answered In God's Timing 220
35. Nearing The New Beginning 226

Conversation 233

FOREWORD

M y brother, Keith, has poured out his heart, mind and soul in writing this book of memories: *This Beautiful Thing Called Church*. He has been transparent, honest, forthright, and soul piercing as he put on paper his genuine meaningful thoughts and memories - those that have really had the most impact upon his life and that of his family. He has expressed so explicitly his feelings that these memories have ushered into his life. His explanations and descriptions at times envelop your emotions and make you cry a river. Other times, they make you laugh and laugh and laugh.

Keith is very straight-forward about telling us the times when his life and priorities were worldly and selfishly oriented, times that led him astray from his spiritual upbringing and close walk with God. However, he is quick to tell us how God intervened at the different junctures and events which he considered to be either bad or great accomplishments achieved. He lets us know that God kept reminding him of who He is and who is really in control of his life journey.

We see that his marriage covenant to his wife Kathy exemplifies obedience to God's plan for marriage between a man and a woman. You feel the real love, dedication, admiration, devotion and endless care giving to her. He states over and over how precious to him she has been and still is. So many memories to cherish and reflect upon, magnifies such a wonderful, joyous life together. We pray that God will allow Kathy to understand some of these memories as he reads this book to her - eyes will light up; she will smile and give a nod to keep reading from *This Beautiful Thing Called Church*.

Keith, your book has certainly touched Toni's and my life. It has caused us to re-focus and continue to be aware of what our priorities in life should always be. That God created us for His purpose, accept Jesus as your Lord and Savior, live a life that will bring honor and glory to Him.

We can do this by daily reading His Holy Scriptures, obeying them and praying consistently. Then tell others about God and how He blesses His children, so that we can be a blessing to others when given that opportunity.

We pray that everyone who reads your book will draw closer to God. If you don't have a personal relationship with God's Son, you should ask Him to come into your life right now and start living for Him. Keith, you have made it so clear why this should be everyone's priority.

Keith, you are and continue to be the best brother anyone could have. I thank God for you and what you stand for. You are a perfect reflection of God's love, that Christian family beliefs do matter, what our priorities should be for eternal life and that leaving a legacy of remembrance for family is so vital for the next generations.

Every day I remember Dad's favorite scripture verse which he quoted in his prayers: "Trust in the Lord with all your heart and lean not on your own understanding; in all your ways acknowledge Him, and He will make your paths straight." Proverbs 3:5-6 (NIV)

May God continue to pour out His righteous blessings upon you, Kathy and your family. This is our daily prayer to the one true and living God that we worship and put our hope, faith and trust in.

Carey Livingston
Denton, TX

MEMORIES

Precious memories, how they linger,
How they ever flood my soul.
In the stillness of the midnight,
Precious sacred scenes unfold.

J. B. F. Wright, 1925

Memories are food for our souls. Memories are the guideposts for our future. Memories complete us as a total person.

Kathy and I had always done everything together. Neither of us had a hobby that took us our separate ways. When she was diagnosed with Alzheimer's, our shared memories became ever so precious. Now only my memory can tell you the wonderful and blessed life we have lived. This will be my effort to record all the memories that come forth. Memories recorded for the pure joy of them still being there to cherish, to laugh or cry at, be embarrassed by and some so vivid one can feel it, smell it, taste it or whatever. I intended for Kathy to be able to read our memories, but it was not to be. Now my best hope is for me to read them to her and pray that occasionally some of my words may bring a smile and brighten her day.

Chapter 1:

THIS BEAUTIFUL THING CALLED CHURCH

※|※

I want to make certain that the meaning of this title "This Beautiful Thing Called Church" is understood. It is not about a beautiful church building. The fellowship of "Born Again" believers in Jesus Christ all over the world is the church, Christ's Church. These believers have blessed our lives by their guidance and fellowship, no matter where we lived or what church building we worshiped in. We are forever grateful to God for that church. If you are not now a part of This Beautiful Thing Called Church, I urge you to learn how you can also be a part of a beautiful thing.

My growing up on a forty-acre farm in rural Mississippi started on March 19, 1939, in the bungalow house with a tin roof where I spent the next eighteen years. I was the second son born to Noel Lee and Mamie Sue McGee Livingston. I was delivered at home by Dr. S. W. Pearson. Their first son, Carey, was born May 23, 1933. He is a major influence in my life, yet there are few early memories because he was six years older. Since he finished high school and left home at the age of sixteen, I was like an only child, as I was only ten years old when he left to attend East Central Jr. College, Decatur, MS. I would also attend there after high school.

My brother, Carey, was six years older.

Mom had an eighth-grade education and Dad less. Dad was the second of six boys. I never knew my Grandfather Livingston, John Davis Sidney Levi Livingston. He died before I was born from an injury in a logging accident. My Grandmother, Mary Alice Chandler Livingston was stooped and didn't have much to say. She dipped snuff. Once a month the Livingston's would go to Grandmother Livingston's after church for Sunday dinner. Everyone brought a covered dish. I would stuff myself with all the delicious food. I had a great time playing with all of my first cousins. Grandfather Livingston owned many acres of timber land that was gradually cleared for cultivation of cotton and corn. He also owned a sawmill and a grocery store. As each son married, he would give them forty acres of his land and a new automobile. That is how my Dad came to own a forty-acre farm and a 1929 Model A Ford.

Mom and Dad were married on the fourth of July, 1929. For their honeymoon they drove the Model A, with a rumble seat, from Louisville to Macon to Columbus to Starkville and back to Louisville. The roads were gravel then, so the trip of one hundred twenty miles took a long day. Every Fourth of July, Dad would tell about making the trip and what an adventure it was because it was the first time either one of them had been out of Winston County. Dad always celebrated their anniversary on the fourth by having watermelon and homemade ice cream. It was my job to turn the freezer for making the ice cream. Mom always made caramel ice cream. She made the caramel by browning regular sugar in a black iron skillet. She made caramel cakes and pies. Caramel was Dad's favorite.

My mother was a McGee, youngest of two daughters of Joseph (Joe) and Kathryn Cockrell McGee. My Mom was only fourteen years old when her mother died of scarlet fever. My Mom's sister, Aunt Madge, was five years older. She got married and moved out, so my Mom did all the housework for her Dad and helped out on their farm. At that time, she had to drop out of school with only an eighth grade education. However, Mother was an avid reader. She literally educated herself. She knew the Bible from Genesis to Revelation. She taught Sunday School for over fifty years. Some of the ladies in her classes had college degrees. She knew all about the great missionaries. William Carey, Corrie Ten Boom and Lottie Moon were her heroes. She saved her pennies all year for the Lottie Moon Christmas Offering. Had she been able to go to high school and college, I believe she would have been a foreign missionary. She loved God and was gifted for telling others about her Savior, Jesus Christ.

After Mom and Dad were married, Grandpa McGee came to live with them. Some of my favorite, earliest memories are me and Grand Pa McGee sitting in the front porch swing, talking and singing church hymns like "When the Roll is Called Up Yonder."

Grand Pa McGee was a faithful Christian. One Sunday, Brother Jody Moore, our preacher came for Sunday dinner. Mother was a fabulous cook. After dinner, Grandpa McGee was sitting in his rocking chair and had a massive heart attack. The doctor came to our house, but in those days, there was nothing he could do for him other than bed rest. Grandpa died the following Friday. He was called on that previous Sunday to pray the benediction, and everyone said that it was the most beautiful prayer they could ever remember him praying. The night after he died, I went to Aunt Madge and Uncle Dick's to spend the night. This was the first time I had stayed away from home at night. They brought Grandpa to our house in the casket. Some men came to sit with the body that night. This was a very sad time for me and my family. I had been close to my Grandpa McGee. He was the only grandparent that I really came to know. I would follow him around the farm as he worked on fences, cut firewood, milked cows and did the many chores that were required to keep food on the table.

My young years were spent growing up on our forty-acre farm. Dad had sold the forty acres given to him by his Dad to the US Government in order to move closer to Mom's sister, Aunt Madge, and brother in law, Uncle Dick. The land Dad sold to the government was almost all timber land except for the few acres Dad and Grandpa McGee had cleared for cultivation. They had been able to plant this small acreage for their food and a few acres for corn and cotton. The farm they purchased in 1935 was already cleared for cultivation except for twenty wooded acres. It was only three miles from the town of Louisville. This would mean that my brother and I would be eligible to attend Louisville Public School. This new location and farm would make all the difference in all of our lives, especially for my brother Carey and me.

My Dad and Grandpa McGee both worked tirelessly on the farm. It was the total source of food and a small amount of income that we had. My mother also worked from daylight to dark. She cooked on a wood burning stove which was an awfully hot job during the summer months in the deep south. She did much of the garden work and all of the canning of wonderful vegetables that we enjoyed all winter.

For several years, in order to have some cash, they milked several cows, morning and evening, storing the milk in a tall heavy steel milk can. Each day the milk truck would run and the milk can had to be hoisted up onto the wooden stand before time for the truck to run. The truck had an open space on the side of the truck bed and the worker riding in the back would slide the can off the wooden stand, almost so fast the truck barely had to stop, only slow down to what we called a crawl.

Dad and Grandpa eventually fenced the entire forty acres. Two major fields were fenced off from the pasture land and the wooded area. The other major field was across the gravel road that passed through the east west width of the farm.

We also became part of a community called Evergreen. As I was growing up, Evergreen Baptist Church and the families that attended became the people in our social life. The community and church is still dear to my heart today. Most of my preschool memories involve the church activities and the Evergreen Church family. It was like a big family. Attendance was usually about forty. We were there every time the church doors opened. We had Sunday School and Worship Service, Sunday night Training Union and Worship Service, and Wednesday night prayer meeting and extra training and social activities like Royal Ambassadors, (RA's) and Girls In Action, (GA's).

I never saw the house where mother grew up. Dad's old home place is restored and today is exactly as it was when I was growing up. The house had two very large rooms on each side of a very wide hallway with a front porch across the entire width of the house. There was a connecting hall at the back of the main house that led to another huge room. This was the kitchen with a giant wood cook stove and a wall of shelves for pots and pans. The dining table was about twelve feet long and had wooden benches on each side. The children got to eat first then we played outside while the grownups had a long relaxing meal together. These times were etched in my memory for these are the only times I was with my cousins. I moved away from Louisville at the age of eighteen and we had only one Livingston reunion about twenty years later. I have kept in touch with a few of my cousins as the years have gone by. My brother and I are the only two of the cousins that went away to college. One other cousin moved to Memphis, but all the others remained in Winston County or nearby counties.

The Livingston Brothers and First Cousins

The Livingston brothers have all passed away. Dad, in 2004, was the last one. The youngest, Uncle Marse, had never married. He lived with and cared for Grandmother Livingston until she died. When he died in 2002, he left the old home place with fourteen acres of land to my brother and me. Over the years, he had sold off many acres and timber to provide a source of income for himself. He had a small Veterans' pension that was not enough to live on.

Carey and I were very surprised that he left the old home place to us. I think it was because our Dad was the only brother still living at the time he died. Uncle Marse had hospital bills he owed, so Carey, as the Executor of the Will decided to sell the place. The person that bought it refurbished it, and it still stands today and looks the same as when we went there for big potluck dinners when we were kids. I am very thankful that it has been preserved.

Our house had four rooms all about the same square footage with a porch across the front. Two front doors led into the two front bedrooms. Carey and I slept in one bedroom and Grandpa McGee the other. Mom and Dad had the back bedroom with the fireplace. The kitchen was in the fourth room. After Grandpa died, I slept in his room and Carey stayed in the bedroom we had shared. When he worked at the Winston Furniture Company after school and on Saturday, he bought a beautiful bedroom set for his bedroom.

Mom had always wanted to improve the appearance of our house both inside and outside. One winter I helped Mom install wallpaper in every room. This would keep the rooms warmer. It was fun picking out the colorful wall papers, but it was no fun hanging the paper. It was easily torn when wet with the glue and it was difficult matching each piece with the last one that was hung. I was best at tacking the gauze to the wall. The paper would not stick to the wooden planks, so the gauze gave something for the paper to adhere to.

I was embarrassed that our car was an old model A and that our green weather boarded, tin roof house did not look nearly as nice as others in our community. We also had an outhouse. Almost everyone in Evergreen community had a bathroom. After I started to school, I had inferiority feelings because of these outward comparisons with our neighbors and especially the townspeople. I know Mom had these same feelings. Dad was always content. He didn't seem to be bothered by the appearance of our house and the fact we had the oldest car around. He didn't buy anything unless he had the money. His first purchase on the installment plan was in 1950 when he bought a 1947 used Chevrolet coup to replace our 1929 Model A. I was a very happy eleven year old boy that day. My poor brother had only the Model A throughout his high school years, for he graduated in 1950 and left for Junior College.

When Dad bought the Chevrolet, his younger brother, Uncle Will, was in the Vicksburg hospital. They thought he had polio. Dad wanted to visit him. He was afraid the old model A would not make the 300-mile round trip. I am certain that is the reason he bought the car. I fell asleep in the back seat on the way back home. Uncle Will died, not from polio, but a brain tumor. Six months prior to his death, a car had rammed the rear of his pickup as he was turning into his driveway. The back of his head took a horrible lick against the metal cab. He had severe headaches. Then he became paralyzed. Polio was prevalent so they treated him for polio.

After his death, his only child, my cousin, Johnny Kirk, actually did have polio. He came very near death, but his life was spared. There were many prayers for him by the Evergreen community as he lay in the hospital. He was crippled in both legs the rest of his life. He was one year younger than me. When I worked at the Five and Dime, he was a disc jockey for WLSM, the Louisville radio station. He and I became pals. I helped him maneuver up steps at school on his crutches. There were no handicap accommodations. We would ride around on Sunday afternoon after church and check out the girls at the A1 Drive In. He started smoking. I had slipped cigarettes from Uncle Dick's house after school a few times before I started working after school. I got started smoking with Johnny Kirk. One day he told me I was not inhaling. So he demonstrated how I was supposed to inhale. After that I was hooked on nicotine, a horrible habit I had for fifty years. I quit once for six months and started back. I tried everything that was suggested for helping to quit. Nothing worked for me for long. I always started back. I finally was able to stop completely after the Doctor said I had the beginning of COPD. Johnny Kirk moved to Memphis after graduating from high school and worked as a disc jockey for a few years. He went to Elvis Presley parties at Graceland. He finally married and settled down. He landed a great job with Delta Airlines Headquarters in Memphis. When Carey or I needed to get on a certain flight that was booked up, he was able to get a seat with his computer and reservation expertise. After I retired, Kathy and I visited him at his home in Memphis a year before he died of lung cancer. He never stopped smoking.

Our oil lamp before we had electricity

I was seven years old before we had electricity, so I remember the many conveniences that came along with electricity. The first convenience that Dad purchased was a refrigerator. It was a used one from the Home Economics Department at the high school. Previously, we had an ice box. A truck would come by twice a week in the summertime and deliver a block of ice made at the Louisville Ice Plant. We would put a cardboard sign out to let the driver know the size of the block of ice we wanted. The ice plant is a vivid memory in my senses of smell, sight and sound. The smell was of wet timbers, the sight was the huge blocks of ice and the ice tongs used to pull the blocks along the wooden flooring and the sound was of the saw that cut the ice blocks into manageable blocks for sale and delivery. There was also the constant sound of an engine running, generating the method used to freeze the water into ice.

Mother was extremely happy to have the refrigerator. The ice cubes made for wonderful sweet tea on the hot summer days in MS. She would use the ice trays to make homemade ice cream, including flavors like caramel and vanilla. When available, she would add strawberries or bananas. The electricity also meant that we no longer had to use the kerosene lamps at night. We now had a single light bulb in the ceiling of each of our four rooms.

The next great convenience was installation of propane gas for heating and cooking. Early in 1947, a gas pipeline was constructed that passed across our farm west to east. The representative for the pipeline met with Mom and Dad to discuss the access to their land for the pipeline right of way. A payment of nine hundred fifty dollars was agreed to for the right of way. This was a windfall for Mom and Dad. Dad was hired for a part time custodial job at the Louisville Post Office in 1941. He only worked twenty hours a week.

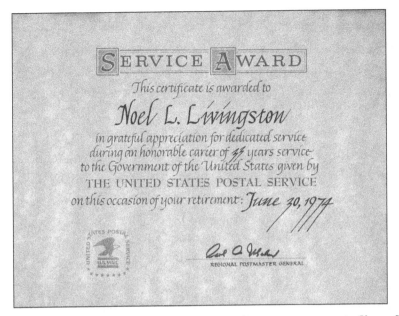

SERVICE AWARD

This certificate is awarded to

Noel L. Livingston

in grateful appreciation for dedicated service during an honorable career of 33 years service to the Government of the United States given by THE UNITED STATES POSTAL SERVICE on this occasion of your retirement: June 30, 1974

REGIONAL POSTMASTER GENERAL

Dad had an honorable career of thirty three years as custodian of the Louisville Post Office.

He continued to farm and produced almost all the food necessary for our family. But with the limited cash income there was little to spend for big ticket items. With the pipeline payment, it was now possible to have propane gas installed with a space heater in each of the four rooms and a new gas stove in the kitchen. This eliminated the need for many manual labor chores. For example, cutting timber, sawing the trees into logs to fit into the fireplace, and splitting wood into small units that would fit into the wood stove. After Grandpa McGee died, I helped Dad saw the trees into firewood. That was really hard work for a kid about six years old. Mom was very, very thankful for the gas stove. I was glad I no longer had to bring in stove wood for cooking and logs for the fireplace. The fireplace was in Mom and Dad's bedroom. Prior to the gas heat, on cold winter mornings, I would jump out of bed and sprint to the fireplace to dress by the fire Dad would have made earlier. Now, I could light my space heater and dress in my room.

With this windfall, Mom and Dad also remodeled the tin roofed bungalow to a regular roof line with roofing shingles. I admit, after they replaced it, I missed the sound of rain on the old tin roof. The brown brick siding was covered with a beautiful light green asbestos siding. With the freshly painted white window trims, our house now looked just as pretty and much like the other homes in the community. They also added six feet across the entire width of the back of the house. This gave Mom a nice pantry off the kitchen, a big screened-in back porch, great for preparing vegetables for canning in summer and a room off their bedroom for a bathroom at some point in the future. All of the remodeling work was done by Dad's younger brothers, Uncle Early and Uncle Marse. They were excellent carpenters. Many years later when Carey and I had the house torn down, the workers said that the section that had been added to the back was the best solidly built they had seen.

Our house after the renovation

The bathroom would have to come later, after I left home. I still had the embarrassing outhouse. There was a valid reason for no bathroom. Mom and Dad wanted one very badly. However, we had a real problem with the well water. It had a high concentration of iron. It was so bad that it turned everything a bright yellow. Our pots and pans, tea pitcher and almost everything used in the kitchen had a yellow glow.

The water problem was finally resolved when there was a project to extend city water out to our acres. The road behind our farm was called Brooksville Road. There were many homes on it. These families convinced the city to extend the water line out their road. When the three families on our road learned about the line coming so close, they immediately began a campaign to get our houses added. It would require payment for the cost of the pipe and labor to bring the line the half mile further. The three families rounded up the two hundred fifty dollars each needed. The day city water came to our house was a celebrated occasion. For many years water had been a problem they could not solve. Dad had several wells dug but they did not always last. Once we actually had to haul water from a spring about a mile from our house while we waited for another well to be dug. The first thing that came with the water was a sink in the kitchen for Mom. The bathroom would come next.

After Dad died in 2004, with no one living in the house, it began to need major repairs. The roof leaked. Mold and mildew was in the carpet. It was at least a hundred years old. Dad had lived in the house seventy years. It was a difficult decision, but Carey and I decided to dismantle it board by board. Ironically, we paid eight hundred dollars to have it razed, the amount Dad had paid for the house and forty acres in 1935. A friend of ours was building a hunting cabin at the time. He used many of the appliances and furniture for his cabin. We were very thankful that some of the old home continued to be useful. A tornado hit the community on April 28, 2014 and demolished every home that was near our old home place. Our house would have been demolished and everything in it scattered for miles. We were so thankful that we made the decision to dismantle it before this happened. Dad's giant pecan trees were destroyed by the tornado. They were over a hundred years old. Dad had sold pecans many times to raise money for our Christmas presents.

Down on the Tree Farm

The entire acreage is now a tree farm that Carey and I have specified in our wills to leave to our boys. Hopefully this will entice them to occasionally check on the home place of our youth. One year on a visit to Louisville I was talking to Pruitt and Jean, our friends that owned the Louisville furniture store. Jean was an artist. We had purchased several of her watercolor paintings. I asked her to do a painting of Dad's house. We had a painting of Kathy's old house where she grew up. Jean did a very nice water-color painting of the house and yard with the trees where I once played. The painting hangs in our den. It reminds me every day of the wonderful memories I have of growing up in that house with parents that loved me and raised me to love God as they did. I am very thankful. How could it be that I now proudly display the house where I grew up but once was embarrassed that it was not as nice as others in the community.

Chapter 2:

THE DUSTY ROAD

◈

The gravel road from the small town of Louisville, Mississippi, county seat of Winston County, cut across the forty-acre farm where I grew up. The road made a ninety degree turn at the northeast corner of the farm where our four room, bungalow house set about thirty five yards off the dusty road. The road went from Louisville to Starkville, the home of Mississippi State University, and was well traveled. It is now a four-lane highway from Jackson to Starkville.

One evening near dusk, as we were sitting down for our supper meal, an empty log truck returning from Louisville after delivering a load of logs to the major industry, D. L. Fair Lumber, lost control as the driver entered the curve going too fast. With a thunderous boom the truck hit the side of the hard clay bank and came to a sudden stop as if it hit a brick wall. The wheels were still turning on the overturned trailer as we rushed the short distance from our house. Dad climbed up on the side of the truck cab laying on its side and yelled into the truck, "are you hurt?" In a low voice, the person responded that he could not move. Those were the only words we heard from the young driver. The sudden stop when the truck hit the embankment caused such a whiplash that it broke the young man's neck and he died quickly. After they removed the body from the truck, they laid him on our front porch. Mother provided some quilts for the handsome black man to lay on. He was in his early twenties. They found a small bag that contained a spool of thread and a stick of penny candy that he had bought for his wife and small child. Later the Evergreen Baptist Church delivered the thread and candy to the mother and child with a donation from the congregation. At that time there were no black members of the congregation, but the church members were good neighbors to everyone that lived in the Evergreen Community.

Almost all the members of Evergreen Church lived on the gravel road. My parents and the church members were the influence during the development of my religious beliefs, any social skills I have, my ethics and all the character traits that make for the foundation of a person's life. Mom and Dad were faithful members of the congregation and lived the best Christian example of anyone I have ever known. We attended church twice on Sunday and every Wednesday night for prayer service and youth activities. Mother was the Sunday School teacher for about ten of us riotous teens. We also attended a training class on Sunday nights called BYTU, Baptist Youth Training Union. Sounds really grown up but it was for us to learn Scripture verses and learn all the important parts of both the Old and New Testament. The study material was produced by the Baptist Sunday School Board. It was very beneficial for me when I studied at Mississippi College night school, working toward my college degree, because I was able to breeze through their required courses in Old and New Testament.

Road named in Dad's honor

Many years passed before a project to pave the road from Louisville to Starkville was approved. The plan called for removing the sharp curve by moving the road and making a gradual turn. It would go across the northwest corner of our forty acres. The state paid eight hundred dollars for the right of way across our farm, the amount Dad had paid for the house and farm in 1935. The new right-of-way that eliminated the curve crossed Dad's farm from the northeast corner as it gradually turned through his fields. The strip of road left coming down to our house from the new route was later paved and named Noel Livingston Road in honor of Dad, whose property was on each side of the two hundred yard street. The old road now ended in front of our house.

Even though the old gravel road and curve is gone, it remains a part of my life because it connected me to my church family. It was a little country Christian fellowship that played a critical role in the development of my life's foundation principles. Of course my parents were the most important influence; however, the congregation's lives and their beliefs confirmed what my parents taught and practiced. There was no reason to doubt my parents. The church family also held me accountable. I knew them and they knew me. I hold a special place in my heart for many of the members. Even though I left at the age of eighteen, I returned on every special occasion that I could to see and talk with the now aging friends. I was always proud to once again be with my parents for the worship service.

Chapter 3:

HAPPY CHILDHOOD

⊱⊰

Growing up on the farm in the Evergreen Community was quite an adventure. And, for the most part, it was a happy time in my life. My preschool age years were centered around attending and participating in the weekly church services and activities. Every year we had a week long Vacation Bible School attended by all the children in the community. We studied the Bible, did arts and crafts and had Bible story time. One year I made a set of bookends, even though we didn't have any books. They were easy to make, and the cut out blocks were furnished. The church services every Sunday and on Wednesday nights gave me opportunities to play with others my age. We didn't play many organized games. We usually played chase or hide and seek. We always got in lots of running and got sweaty, but if there was a breeze it would help cool us off.

My Mother's only sister, Aunt Madge, lived a short quarter mile from us. Aunt Madge's daughter, Dixie, lived even closer on the farm next to ours. Dixie's daughter Linda was four years younger than me. She was a regular tom boy. Her Dad's parents had some Indian blood. Linda was as tough or tougher than I was. We played toy cars, cowboy and outlaws and even football. One day we were riding our bikes on the gravel road and my dog Duck darted in front of Linda's bike. It wrecked Linda, and she went sprawling across the gravel, scrapping the skin from her face, arms, hands and legs. She was a sight, but her Mom doctored her up and all the scratches healed nicely without any scars. I am sure it was very painful when it happened.

One year Santa Claus brought me a Red Ryder BB gun. Linda and I would often get mad with each other, and she would go home but would come back after a short cooling off period. She was trying out my BB gun, and I dared her to shoot me, declaring it would not hurt. I was standing on the front porch, and the instant she shot I fell out onto the ground and didn't move when she asked if I was hurt. She was certain I was faking, so she grabs her bike and goes home. While she is away, I go into the kitchen and get some ketchup and put it on my shirt. I watch for her and when she starts back, I lay back down with the part of my shirt with ketchup showing. When she sees this, she flies back home, and before I could get out to her house to explain that I was OK, she and her Mom headed to our house. I got in big trouble for that act.

Over the years Mom gave me a few whelps with a small peach tree switch. All of them were when I truly deserved it. There was never a time when I doubted that Mom and Dad loved me, and I knew I loved them. Discipline and love and honor for our parents are all covered in the Holy Scripture.

All my time was not spent playing and having fun. There were always chores that needed to be done, especially in the summer time with the large garden producing a bountiful crop of fruits and vegetables that needed to be preserved and canned for winter. At this time, we did not have electricity, so we had no freezer. I helped Mom pick vegetables like peas, string beans and butter beans, then shell them. Some days in summer we worked almost all day, for it was time consuming work. It was also my job to wash the jars that had to be spotless and then soaked in scalding hot water to make certain all bacteria was removed. It was always a joy to hear the jars pop at night after a day of canning. That meant that the jar seals were sealing correctly. We never were sick from any of the hundreds of meals we had from the wonderful canned vegetables. You cannot imagine how hot it was in the kitchen during summer when all of the canning was taking place and the wood stove was going full blast all day.

One job I hated every summer was blackberry picking. These were wild blackberries that grew on the briers growing on the fences that surrounded the corn fields. I always got chiggers on me that itched for days. But I dearly loved the blackberry jelly we had all year. The jelly on one of Mom's hot, buttered, homemade buttermilk biscuits was a special treat on a cold winter morning.

Another duty for me was to bring in the stove wood from outside and keep it in a box near the stove. A few times I helped Dad saw up a tree cut down for firewood and stove wood. About ten acres of our farm was wooded with growing hardwood and pines. It was a major and dangerous task to fell the tree. Then it was hard work to saw it into manageable sections in order to be able to load it onto the wagon and haul it to the house. There it was split into smaller sections that would fit inside either the stove or fireplace. This was backbreaking muscle building labor which my Dad did for many years. I can only imagine how thankful he was when he was able to afford to buy a propane gas tank and pay the plumber to run the gas pipes for installing the space heaters for each room. Then Mom was overjoyed to be able to have a gas stove. It still got hot in the kitchen, but it was much less heat than the wood stove.

My brother, Carey, and I always shared one chore. We shared it because it was so tough on your hands. The corn in our corn crib had to be shucked then shelled by our hands. This would quickly make the hands raw. You would not last long if you had dish pan hands. When Carey got a job after school and on Saturday, the first thing that he bought was a corn sheller. You entered the ear of corn into the sheller then turned the handle and the sides of the sheller stripped the kernels right off the cob, untouched by human hands. He still has that corn sheller as a reminder of what farm life was like. The shelled corn was taken to the grist mill and ground into corn meal used for making corn bread. We had corn bread for both dinner (noon) and supper (night). We always had biscuits for breakfast.

Another job for me when I got strong enough was to take the slop bucket of liquid and food waste to feed the hogs. This bucket was the modern-day garbage disposal. It was left over foods, of which there was very little, trimmings and peelings from foods that were prepared for cooking. A purchased special feed for hogs was added with water to make for what seemed to be a very delicious meal for the hogs, for they pushed and shoved each other furiously trying to get their fair share. The hogs were a vital item of food for our family. We had a smokehouse where the meat was smoked for a few days after being killed and dressed. Then it was salted down in the salt box and stored all year. Mom could go to the smokehouse and cut off a portion of ham or side of bacon when it was needed.

My brother was six years older so most of his chores were to help Dad in the fields plowing and hoeing the weeds from around the corn and picking cotton. I helped some in the fields putting nitrate of soda around the young corn. We would try to time this task before a rain. The rain and soda would grow the corn fast. Most of my work was inside helping Mom with the canning. I also waxed our wood floors when the preacher was coming for Sunday dinner.

My preschool years were a little of everything and never boring. With my chores and Linda my playmate from next door always coming over to play, I was never without something to do. Any spare time I had I would explore the woods or wade and play in the stream that ran across our farm, especially after a rain. After dark, I might be chasing after lightning bugs to store them in a glass jar. Some lazy day if I had nothing to do, I would lie on the pine straw under a pine tree and watch the billowing clouds so common every day down south and think about God and heaven and our life and all my family and friends. Most nights I was fast asleep the minute my head hit the pillow. This was a good thing because the nights could be awfully hot without air conditioning during the southern summers.

One of the happiest memories of my young life happened on May 8, 1945. I could feel the hot dust on my bare feet as I ran as fast as I could the hundred yards to Uncle Dick and Aunt Madge's house. I bounded up the steps of their sturdy wooden frame house with a wide front porch that seemed to always need painting. I was about to deliver the most important news I had known in my six years. When I got there, I was so out of breath I couldn't say anything for a minute. They thought something terrible had happened. Meanwhile my Mom was speed walking to tell the news to Dad and Grandpa McGee who were plowing in the field. Mom and I had been listening to the battery radio, we didn't have electricity at this time, when the announcer interrupted the program with the telegraph wire message that the Germans had just surrendered. The war in Europe was over. Our radio was our major entertainment. I remember well the enjoyment of listening to the funny programs; Lum and Abner, Amos and Andy and Ozzie and Harriet. We also never missed the scary programs; The Squeaking Door and The Shadow Knows. Mom loved to listen to Arthur Godfrey and the soap operas; The Guiding Light and Just Plain Bill. We all liked to listen to the Grand Ole Opera on Saturday night. Dad and Grandpa McGee listened to Gabriel Heater, who reported the news every night. When I finally caught my breath, I announced the wonderful news to Aunt Madge and Dixie. They were overjoyed and immediately headed to our house. They had to hear the news for themselves. Dixie's husband, Billy, was with Patton's Third Army throughout Patton's long successful campaigns through North Africa, Italy, and France. The last news they had from Billy was that they were headed into Germany. They were worried sick hearing that the Germans had launched a last desperate battle known as the Battle of the Bulge. It had been a month since they had heard from Billy.

The church family and all of us prayed constantly for Billy's safety. We learned later that it was a miracle that Billy's life was spared. His 105 millimeter artillery gun buddy James, that had been with him the entire war, was hit and killed by shrapnel as he stood next to Billy in the horrific Battle of the Bulge.

There was no more work that day. Uncle Dick even came home from his job as a train engine mechanic at the GM&O train station in Louisville. That evening everyone brought a covered dish for a thanksgiving meal and special thankful prayers for the end of the long terrible war. It was several weeks before we learned that Billy was alive and well.

After the war, Billy and his Dad built a house across the road from our farm. Uncle Dick sold Billy and Dixie about half of his acres. Billy worked hard farming the land. It was all manual labor. He worked alone from daylight to dark. He first had cotton and corn crops. Then he added milk cows and for many years he ran a sizable dairy operation. He later purchased more land for hay and corn. After several years he purchased a tractor and many mechanized farm implements that made his work easier. He never talked about the war and he always worked alone. I wonder how difficult it was for him to carry all the terrible bloodshed and death he had witnessed in his young life. It seemed he drowned all of his heart breaking memories in hard work. To me his life being spared was a very significant answer to prayer in my young life. There would be many more.

Chapter 4:

MAKING MOLASSES AND KILLING HOGS

⊱⊰

Two occasions on our farm were treated as celebrations like Thanksgiving and the Fourth of July. Of course we celebrated those holidays too, as well as Christmas; but the Fourth, Thanksgiving and Christmas were celebrated by everyone. Hog killing and molasses making were our own private time of festivities. These activities required hard labor and a multitude of skills. Skills that had been passed down to Mom and Dad by their parents plus some self-teaching thrown in. Hog killing day and molasses making day were big holidays for me, because I got to stay home from school and help the grownups.

Hog killing required a gutsy call to pick the best day for the job. It had to be the coldest day, near freezing, which was not that often in the deep south. Once the decision was made, the activity started at day break. Dad shot the hog with his rifle, cut its throat to bleed it, then hauled it to the edge of the yard by the smokehouse where a lift made from a sapling tree stood ready like a gallows for hanging the hog up by its front legs. It was homemade using a tall, strong sapling tree that was nailed to two legs. A big drum dug into the ground at a forty five degree angle was filled with scalding hot water which was furnished from a big black steel pot with a blazing fire burning around it. One of my jobs was to keep that fire going so that plenty of boiling hot water was ready for cleaning the hog inside and out. After the hog was sloshed in and out of the big drum, the hair was scraped off with knives. This sloshing effort took two strong men to pull the four hundred pound hog in and out of the drum. The neighbors always pitched in and helped one another on hog killing day. After all the hair was removed and the skin was clean, the hog was lifted up head first by the homemade lift, with the two front legs tied to a single tree attached to the lift. (A single-tree was used to hitch a plow horse to a plow. A doubletree would hitch two horses to a plow.) This was a beauty to behold. I usually disappeared for I did not care to witness this next procedure. Dad, with the precision of a surgeon and a very sharp knife, opened the hog's stomach and removed the intestines and vital organs, heart, lungs, liver and even the brains. The expression is that everything about the hog is used except the squill. The intestines are known as chitterlings. These I never could stand to eat or smell cooking. Some folks even pickle the hog's feet, but we never did that. The intestines were cleaned then boiled then fried and were the main course at someone's house that held a chitterling supper. We did not host one of them, but Mom and Dad would give the chitterlings to a neighbor and then attend the supper.

The vital organs, heart, liver and lungs had to be cooked the same day as the hog killing. They were not suitable for the smoke-house and preserving like the other hog meats. Mother would prepare a huge dinner for the workers using her special recipes for these vital organs. I liked the liver, but I was not a fan of the heart and lungs. Mom served the brains at breakfast. They were similar to eggs in looks and taste. After the hog was washed down, it was taken down and placed on a wooden table near the smokehouse. Dad stood at the table and carved the hog into the major sections. The two hams were the back legs, two shoulders, the front legs, the ribs, loin and many pounds of lean and fat that would be chopped and made into sausage. The fat next to the skin was cut and cooked in a pot outside. These crisp pieces of fat were called cracklings. The grease from cooking them became lard when it hardened and was used for frying foods. My main job every hog killing was turning the sausage grinder that ground the lean meat into hamburger like meat for sausage. The sausage was stuffed into the casings (intestines) and smoked in the smokehouse to preserve them. They were very good for breakfast on a cold morning.

The other major sections of the hog were smoked in the smokehouse for several days. In the center of the smoke house a small fire in a steel pot was kept smoldering so it would produce smoke. After the meat was smoked, it was moved to the salt box in the smokehouse and salted down. This preserved the meat and it was used all year round. Mom would go to the smokehouse and cut off the portion she needed for the day; ham, bacon or sausage. The pork loin, like you see in the grocery store, was the favorite cut of meat. It was served on special occasions, usually fried for breakfast and served with Mom's delicious biscuits and gravy.

Our Smoke House

These are the highlights of hog killing day. It is amazing how much work and skill was required to accomplish this enormous task successfully. It was indeed a celebration when all was accomplished without any major cuts or pulled muscles. This wonderful food source served the family all year long.

One other holiday celebration unique to our family was the occasion for making molasses. In addition to killing hogs, making molasses was another school day that I could skip and help the grownups. Sugar cane was harvested in the late fall, just at the peak of maturity for the sweet juice of Dad's prized Louisiana blue-ribbon sugar cane.

Both Mom and Dad were skilled, self-taught gardeners. Their huge garden and what Dad called his truck patches in the fields, contained all the wonderful vegetables that we enjoyed all year long, both freshly picked and those that were canned when in season. Their garden produced from early spring to late fall until the first frost.

Of all the delicious foods that they grew, I think Dad was most proud of his blue-ribbon cane. It was not something you could go to the store or farmer's cooperative and buy every year for planting. In order to preserve the cane from year to year, Dad would bury a dozen or more stalks in a shallow grave, cover them with pine straw and empty burlap feed bags. Then, in the spring he cut the preserved stalks at the joints making usually six joints about six inches in length. He planted these and from each joint several stalks of cane would sprout, similar to the way potatoes sprout when planted. In the fall, when the cane was ready for harvesting, Dad cut the cane down and we would strip the long, slender leaves from the stalks. The leaves had sharp edges that would cut so you needed gloves for this job.

On the morning for making molasses, the cane stalks were loaded onto the wagon. The plow horse, Baldy, and our small horse, Old Red, were hitched to the wagon and we headed to Uncle

Oakley's, Dad's older brother, that lived three miles from us on the gravel road near the Evergreen Baptist Church. Uncle Oakley owned the only cane squeezer for miles around. You had to make an appointment to get your day locked in. The cane stalks were put into a press of two round steel wheels that turned as the result of an attachment to the wheels that ran to the mule as the mule circled round and round turning the wheels and squeezing the juice from the stalks as they were fed into the wheels. The juice was routed into a spout that dropped it into a large metal pan about six feet long and four feet wide and three inches deep. The pan had a hot wood fire burning under it that was kept burning, keeping the juice boiling and producing one of the sweetest smelling aromas you could ever experience. A long handled paddle was used to constantly stir the bubbling juice to prevent it from sticking. The juice got thicker and thicker as it continued to boil, a sample was taken and dropped into a bucket of cold water to test how thick the syrup would be when it cooled. When it tested the exact thickness it needed to be, it was drained into half gallon tin buckets and sealed.

This wonderful, high fructose cane syrup was a special treat for breakfast every morning, served with Mom's wonderful buttermilk biscuits and brown gravy. I would mix all three together. It didn't look very appetizing, but it was delicious. I still have that dish on occasion. It brings back those fond memories of the molasses making holiday. I can see Dad's proud smile when he got those molasses just the right thickness so that they would pour very slowly and were not runny.

I guess all young boys believe their Dads can do anything. I believed both my Mom and Dad could do anything. Dad was a provider. He worked from daybreak to sundown, then rested on Sunday. He could repair anything and made some of the farm implements he used. He could also cook. For two years, he cooked for himself and Mom after she had a stroke. Then, after she died, he cooked for himself for many years and continued to maintain a beautiful garden until he was well into his nineties. He could also make county fair, award-winning peanut brittle using the wonderful blue-ribbon cane syrup he had made and adding the peanuts he had grown.

Mom was an exceptional cook simply because she had no recipes. The Evergreen cookbook has none of her great recipes because she never had written any of them down. She cooked completely from memory without measuring cups or spoons. She also was a seamstress. She used a sewing machine with a foot peddle. She made her own dresses. She made shirts for me from flour sacks. She made quilts in the winter time when there was no garden work to be done. I have several of her beautiful hand stitched quilts that I cherish. Dad would hang the quilting frame, which was the size for a quilt for a double bed, in their bedroom during the winter months. With ropes on the four corners of the frame it could be let down when Mom was ready to do some quilting.

I am thankful and blessed that my Mom and Dad's Christian faith and work ethic set the example for me. I am currently trying to live the example set by my Dad as I now care and cook for Kathy and myself.

Chapter 5:

A LIFE SPARED

⇥⇤

My life's story would have been completely different had God not spared the life of my brother, Carey. It was a warm summer afternoon when I was four years old. My big brother was six years older than me. The Evergreen Baptist Church summer revival was held this week. Our cousin Pharris had come home from the revival to spend the afternoon with Carey. They were the same age. They were strolling through the pasture, after checking out the snake population at our small, muddy farm pond that Dad had dug with what looked like a big two handled shovel pulled by our plow horse. There was usually a snake or two sunning themselves on the bank. As they came up behind Baldy, our very old, gentle plow horse, Carey, thinking he would show Pharris how gentle the old horse was, slapped him hard on his hip. The horse had lost his hearing, so he did not hear Carey and Pharris approaching. He instinctively kicked up his left foot, landing his hoof squarely on Carey's right jaw and breaking it in two places. The break was the width of the horse's hoof. The Doctor remarked that had this deadly strike landed just inches higher, it would have surely caused either death or severe brain damage.

Riding Baldy with my dog, Duck, tagging along

After Pharris was able to assist Carey to his feet, they hobbled the short distance into our yard. By now both were covered in blood. I was very young and can only recall that Mother was out of the house screaming and crying at the top of her lungs. She yelled for me to get some towels. That is all I can recall that I did. I probably stayed as far away from the bloody scene as I could. At this point, all that was available was for Mother to try and stop the bleeding. We had no phone. Dad had the car at work in town. Our closest neighbor was at work. I am sure Mom was praying to

God for help. Even though the gravel road was not heavily traveled at that time of the afternoon, a lone car was approaching and Pharris flagged it down to ask for help. It was none other than Mr. Parks, a member of Evergreen Baptist Church. Incidentally, some fifteen years later, this same Mr. Parks would become Carey's father-in-law. Mr. Parks took Mother and Carey to the Louisville Hospital, the only hospital in our small town. It was owned by two doctors, Crawford and Hickman. Neither were surgeons. Both did general practice. Together they worked to patch up Carey's jaw, stabilizing the floating section of jaw bone as best they could. Then they wrapped his entire head so the bone could not move. They applied the customary cat gut stitches to the ugly gashes on his young face. His jaw bone healed perfectly. He had only a very slight scar that eventually disappeared as his face matured. The prayers of Mom, Dad and the whole Evergreen Church community were answered, because the outcome of this dreadful accident could have been much, much worse.

Carey was in the hospital several days, and I remember going to visit him once. His entire head was in a big white bandage, with only an opening for his mouth and eyes. He only had liquids until his jaw healed enough to eat solid food. You ask him today what he ate, and he'll say he didn't miss a meal. Thankfully, Dad had started working at the Post Office and was enrolled in the available medical insurance. I am sure the hospital bill for this accident was substantial.

Carey did not get to attend any more of the revival services that summer. But, the very next revival service he attended, he went down when the invitation was given and accepted Jesus Christ as his personal Savior and joined the church.

Carey became my informal mentor, especially for my various career choices. The example he set and the guidance he often provided, set the stage for the many opportunities for me to take advantage of throughout my life. Due to our age difference, we were never play mates as we were growing up. He became someone that I looked up to and wanted to emulate. As a result of his work ethic, honesty and dependability, many times it was easy for me to follow his same career choices. He always had a strong desire to excel. He learned of a high school program for taking extra subjects so he could complete high school in three years. He graduated from high school at the age of sixteen and left home for East Central Junior College (ECJC), Decatur, MS. He earned his total cost by working in the cafeteria and by driving Miss Sullivan, the Psychology Teacher, to many places in Mississippi. I was ten years old when Carey left home.

Before leaving home, he had worked after school helping the school custodian sweep the classrooms and halls. Then at the age of 14, he was hired by Mr. Redd, the owner of Winston

Furniture, to work after school and on Saturday. Mr. Redd was also the Manager of the Walker Stores Five and Dime. When I was fourteen, Mr. Redd hired me to work after school and Saturdays at the Five and Dime. I worked there until I finished High School at the age of eighteen. My first pay was thirty five cents an hour.

Meanwhile, Carey, after graduating from ECJC, worked for Walker Stores at their Headquarters in Columbia, MS. At this time the Korean Conflict resulted in his being eligible for the military draft. Rather than waiting for his draft notice, he joined the MS National Guard in Philadelphia, MS, then volunteered for active duty. He then served two years at Fort Knox, KY. His assignment was with Third Armored Division Personnel Office Chief Administrator. It gave him great training and experience that greatly benefited later career opportunities. When he returned from active duty, he was hired by the MS National Guard, promoted to Second Lt., and worked at the Philadelphia, MS, National Guard Armory.

During this time, he learned that if my parents signed for me, I could join the National Guard at the age of seventeen and a half. They did, and I became a soldier while still a junior in high school.

35

This opportunity for me, created by my brother, resulted in my having a very successful career of thirty-two years in the National Guard and Army Reserves. Every Monday night after working after school at the Five and Dime, I rode with a fellow guardsman to Philadelphia for training. All my study and homework were done during a one hour study hall period during my school day.

Concerned about a job after I graduated from high school that would enable me to save for my first year at ECJC, Carey now working full time with the National Guard, obtained an assignment for me to train at Fort Jackson, SC at the clerk typist school. A week after graduating from HS, I was on a Greyhound bus traveling from Louisville to Fort Jackson, SC. It was a long day and night trip, for the bus stopped in many towns along the way.

Just as I was completing my first year at ECJC, low and behold, I received a formal letter from W E Walker Stores offering me a job as Assistant Manager for their store in Forest, MS. It was not a difficult decision. Dad's hours at the Post Office had been cut from four a day to two, cutting his salary in half. I had a good job at ECJC working at the snack bar in the student center that payed most of my college expenses. This added to the money I saved during the summer at Fort Jackson and paid for my first year of college. However, I knew Mom and Dad were not able to sup-port me for another three years of college. I also had no job lined up for the summer. Besides, at nineteen years old, I would be the Assistant Manager of a store. What an ego booster to jump from stock boy/janitor to Assistant Manager. My brother had worked for them before having to leave for the Army. His recommendation that I join the National Guard had already proved to be a great decision. So, how could I go wrong following in his footsteps. This chosen career could be a great opportunity.

God's hand was leading me in this decision as a result of my parents' prayers. My two years in Forest, MS were critical years for my maturing and also for the major decisions I made while I was working there. These decisions affected and directed my career and life choices. They have resulted in the most blessed and happy life that I never could have dreamed I would have.

By now Carey was graduating from Mississippi State University after attending night school. He then married Betty, the daughter of Mr. Parks, the man that had stopped and delivered the horse kicked victim to the hospital. They bought a house in Philadelphia, MS where he settled into his promising career working for the MS National Guard. One of Carey's co-workers at the Guard had a brother that was Customer Engineering Manager with IBM in Little Rock, Arkansas. In conversation, Carey learned there was an opening on the IBM Administration Staff for which Carey would be well qualified. He interviewed for the job and was hired. At that time IBM was the premiere company in the US and the world. The stock was the darling of the DOW. This was in early 1961, and I was at ECJC attending my second year of Junior College. As soon as I learned that Carey was hired by IBM, immediately my career goal was to also become an employee for IBM.

Only after many years did I realize what a significant influence my brother had been in many of my major life decisions. I strongly believe that we have enjoyed the tremendous success in our lives because of our parents' prayers and our own faith and prayers for God to guide our decisions in life. I believe with all my heart, that because of God's plan for our lives, He spared the life of my brother when he was kicked by our old plow horse, Baldy, on that beautiful summer day in the pasture of our farm. We have both been blessed beyond anything we could have ever imagined when we started out from our humble beginnings.

Chapter 6:

A MISERABLE SUMMER

🔹

I am not sure what it was all about with my brother and me regarding animals. It was a horse for him one terrible summer. For me it was a dog for my miserable summer. My inferiority complex that developed as a youngster had become less bothersome as I completed the fourth grade. When I first started school, I was keenly aware that our house and old 1929 model A car were not as nice and up to date as most of our neighbors. I was especially sensitive that we had no running water and thus no bathroom. Instead, we had an outhouse. Our baths were with a washcloth and pan of soapy water.

My fourth grade teacher, Mrs. Legan, was the best teacher I had during my twelve years at Louisville High School. She took a personal interest in each student. She taught us well and we learned a lot. She read Treasure Island to us after lunch each day. This kept us alert during the sleepy period after playing hard at lunch. My grades were great, and I was really feeling good about myself. I was looking forward to an enjoyable summer.

When I first saw him, the mid-size black dog was standing under the tall oak tree at the edge of our yard next to the gravel road. He didn't move as I walked toward him. Neither did he wag his tail or growl. He seemed to be ill, and his eyes were very red and watery. Since he seemed friendly enough, I reached out and rubbed his back ever so lightly. Suddenly he bolted away at a fast run into our pasture. I thought no more about it. People often left their unwanted dogs and cats at a spot past our house that was out of sight of any houses. When these strays would come around, Dad instructed us to never feed them and soon they would leave.

That afternoon, our neighbor spotted a dog in our pasture running in circles, barking and foaming at the mouth. He suspected the dog was rabid. He got his rifle and killed the dog. This is when my Mother wanted to know if that was the dog she saw me pet that morning. My yes answer sent Mother into a frenzy. She asked the neighbor if he was sure the dog was rabid. He said the only way to know for sure was to send the dog to Mississippi State University (MSU) and have it tested. The test came back positive, the dog was infected with rabies. Since I had only slightly touched the dog and had no open wounds it was very unlikely that I could be infected. However, we must have Dr. Pearson, our family doctor, give us his advice. As a precaution, I would need the preventive treatment. Rabies was fatal so we could not take a chance.

The prevention treatment was a series of shots given daily in my back. The shot caused temporary pain but was not much more than a regular shot. It just took longer to get the medication injected. The first one was scary, but I guess I got used to taking them. After half of the shots had been given, I developed a very high fever, was nauseated and dehydrated. Again, Mother was in a panic. She was certain I had developed rabies and was about to die. By the time we were at the Doctor's office, my fever had reached the point that I was delirious. I had never ever been that way before. Doctor Pearson put me to bed in his small clinic and began to run tests to determine the cause for my fever. Mom and Dad stayed with me all night. They treated my dehydration and got my fever under control. I began to improve. The test confirmed that I had a serious case of malaria fever. Those mosquito bites had taken their toll. I was started on the strongest prescription for my age that he could give of quinine. In a couple of days, I was back home and beginning to be my ole self. What an ordeal we had been through. Mom and Dad were thankful to God that I would be fine.

By the end of summer, my complexion was a color between a lemon and orange, pale yellow. I would be so embarrassed to enter school looking like this. I felt my old inferiority complex returning. It would also be rather awkward trying to explain how lucky I was to have malaria fever rather than what we all thought for sure was rabies.

By now, I think Mom and Dad were ready to ask Evergreen Baptist Church members to keep Carey and myself on their prayer list permanently. Never again would I pet a stray dog or cat.

Chapter 7:

REVIVAL

⟫⊹⟪

Every summer, the Evergreen Baptist Church held a revival. A
visiting preacher would come and conduct both morning and
evening services. The year I was twelve, James Fancher, a young
Seminary student, conducted our revival and his new bride sang
the song specials each service. He was a terrific preacher with
simple messages straight from the Bible. His delivery reminded
everyone of Billy Graham, with the Bible often raised in one
hand as emphasis. One afternoon, after attending the service that
morning, I told Mother that I felt God was asking my heart to
respond to the invitation and go down and join the church. I had
been in Sunday School and church all of my life, and I knew all
about Jesus Christ and the Bible. Mother sat down with me at the
kitchen table and took me step by step through what it means to
accept Jesus into my life and live for Him. She questioned me to
determine if I understood that I was a sinner and needed to repent
of my sins. She asked me to ask God's forgiveness and ask Jesus
to come into my heart and live the rest of my life with Him as the
Lord of my life. After I had responded to all of her questions hon-
estly and from my heart, she asked me to pray and ask for Christ
to come into my heart and allow the Holy Spirit to be my guide for

the rest of my life. At that moment, I was filled with a joy and a feeling of complete freedom from all my sins. In thankful humbleness, I shed tears of joy as I hugged my Mom. That night I joined the Evergreen Baptist Church and was later baptized in Mitchell's Pond along with others that had recently accepted Christ.

The Evergreen Baptist Church

That was the happiest and most positive of all my summers when I was young. In a short two years, I would spend my summers working at Walker's Five and Dime on main street, Louisville. My attendance at Revivals became a rare occurrence. In fact, after graduation from high school, church attendance was not a priority, which I regret.

The National Guard changed the training drills from four Monday nights a month to all day Sunday once a month. This took me away from church once a month. At college, I slept in on Sunday. I did attend the Baptist Student Union social on Sunday nights and enjoyed the fellowship of Christian friends. When I worked two years in Forest, MS, my excuse for not attending church was that

I didn't know anyone. As often as I could afford the gas, I would visit Mom and Dad for Mom's great cooking and go to church with them at Evergreen. That was a point in my advancing career that church and my relationship with Christ was at its lowest. I am thankful that a big wake up from God put me back on the right path. Later, as parents, and as our two boys grew older, we made sure they attended Sunday school and worship service. We set the example for them by always attending with them. I know it is critical that children learn about the Bible and Christianity and that their circle of friends endorse and confirm what they are taught at home and church.

During those years that my Christianity was lacking zeal, there was never a time when I was not aware of my sins and my personal prayer was that of asking for forgiveness and thanking God for all that he was doing for me and my family. I believe that my parents' strong faith and daily prayers to God on my behalf prevented my life from ever straying very far from my personal relationship with Jesus Christ. I also know that often God was directing events in my life that at the time I may not have recognized as His doing, but later saw that He must have always had my best interest in mind.

During my early years in school we had a devotional and short Bible reading first thing each morning in home room. We used the little devotional magazine *Open Windows*, and each student took a turn at reading the devotion and Scripture. This simple act of worship with my peers to start the day was acknowledgment that the Bible was important for instruction in how to live our lives. When young, our peers can be a significant influence on our decisions. When my fellow classmates participated in the simple devotional reading each day, it confirmed for me what I was taught at home and church. Since prayers and this type of devotional time were removed from schools, I believe our society has suffered. Our society continues to become less and less of a loving people with faith in God and belief in the Bible as God's Holy Word. It is evident every day that a life lived by a true Christian based on the teachings in the Bible is a life that has meaning, purpose, and above all love for their fellow man.

My acceptance of Jesus Christ as my personal Savior at the summer revival many years ago at Evergreen Baptist Church is a vivid and lasting memory. There have been many times that God has brought revival in my heart and put me back into a loving relationship with Him. I am thankful for all of those revivals. We may stray but God never strays. He is always there forgiving and loving just as we are there for our children. That sums it up quite well. Once we are a child of God, we know how it all ends so we can face tomorrow no matter what tomorrow may bring. Given our current circumstances, this means everything. Hallelujah and Amen.

Chapter 8:

SCHOOL DAYS

⋈

My twelve years at Louisville High School (LHS) were very important to my life in many, many ways. School gave me a steady diet of knowledge, gave me self-confidence, reduced my inferiority complex, and gave me almost 100% of the skills that I have needed and used throughout my life. I received additional professional training in the military and in management classes in my IBM career. In addition, the two years of Community College and the college degree I earned by attending night school for four years, added significantly to my skills that have enabled my career successes. I am very thankful for the outstanding foundation of my education provided by this small-town school. At the time, no outside government agency that I am aware of dictated any requirements for the teachers and administrators. The school was completely managed by the local townspeople. It makes me sad to hear the comment today that "our schools are failing" or the statement that the US schools are falling further behind other countries in producing a well-educated and skilled society. I credit my great education to the fact that the teachers were dedicated with a sincere desire for the students to learn, the discipline they required in their classroom, and the competitive grading system that pushed us all to do our very best.

Starting with fourth grade, LHS gradually developed my skills in reading, writing, English, math, accounting, typing, history and literature. The teachers not only taught their course of expertise, but also gave guidance for living, such as being truthful, honest and disciplined. In fourth grade, Mrs. Legan had us memorize the multiplication table through twelve time twelve. I still use that every day. Mr. Edwards in sixth grade taught us to do math in our head by rounding the problem to tens and responding with the answer without ever using paper or pencil. And Mrs. Duncan had us memorize Lincoln's "Gettysburg Address." Mother helped me with that difficult task. I did it so well that Mrs. Duncan sent me to the Principal's office for me to recite it to him. I think I must have looked like Lincoln, tall and skinny. History was reading, testing and understanding the reasons behind events of historical significance. We also learned the impact of leaders' decisions, both negative and positive, on the events that changed the course of a country or society.

I was not a straight A student by a long shot. I usually made B's with a few A's and C's. I didn't do any extra studying, only what was required. At age fourteen, in eighth grade, I landed a job working after school and on Saturdays at Walker's Five and Dime. The Manager, Mr. Redd, had hired Carey to work at his furniture store when Carey was fourteen also. Carey's model as a good worker was instrumental in my getting the job. Most of my homework was done during the one hour study period we had each day. Also, since we did not have a TV at home, I did any additional homework needed after I got home. My job and my grades in school gave me self-confidence.

The first Christmas after I started working, it was a thrill for me to be able, for the first time, to buy Christmas presents for Mom and Dad. As I walked down the sidewalk with my packages, the speakers at Winston Furniture were playing the Christmas carol, Silver Bells. Every Christmas when I hear it played, it brings back the joyful feeling I had that Christmas.

Another enjoyable benefit resulted from having the after school job. I no longer had to take a bag lunch to school. Each day at lunch break I would dash to Peggy's Grill about a half mile from school and chow down on a delicious hot dog for ten cents and a hamburger for fifteen with a coke for six cents. For a total of One dollar and fifty five cents each week, I had my favorite meal. The mile round trip at a fast clip gave me some needed exercise.

My working after school job enabled me to make a very important decision. I had a cavity in a front tooth that began to show. I didn't want it to get worse, so I made my first ever dental appointment with Doctor Griffin, whose office was next door to the Post Office. After a thorough examination, to my dismay, he explained that I had a mouth full of cavities that needed to be taken care of. Since I had never brushed my teeth consistently every day, and had eaten our sugar cane syrup almost daily, the cavities were a natural result. He estimated it would cost three hundred dollars for all the needed fillings. After I explained I could not afford to have the work done, he suggested I could pay some each month. Each week I earned seven dollars and fifty cents, minus Social Security tax. We agreed I would pay ten dollars a month. I went to the dentist weekly until he had repaired all of my huge cavities. The total cost was two hundred and sixty dollars. I paid off the entire bill before I finished high school. It was a very wise decision for a fourteen year old. Every dentist that has looked in my mouth over the years commented on the remarkable quality of the dental work. I would tell them the story of how it came to be. Our little country town was certainly blessed to have such a very highly skilled dentist.

Both school and work were factors in reducing my inferiority complex. In my Junior and Senior years, I was elected to the Student Council. The council was comprised of two representatives from each of the classes 9 thru 12. We were responsible for publishing the Student Handbook. It contained the rules and punishments for any violations of the rules. It also described dress code and how we should respect our teachers and classmates. I wonder if the schools still adopt a Student Handbook. I believe it would help address the bullying problems in schools today.

My twelve years at LHS were happy, enjoyable and productive. I returned to each of our class reunions. Seeing my classmates again and feeling that they were all my friends was a powerful reminder that the twelve years we had been together were so very, very important and wonderful. Our class as a whole has been very successful, and I believe in most cases they have set a valuable citizenship and Christian life example for their children and grandchildren. It has been a blessing to keep up with the lives of many of them.

My only personal regret is that I did not go back and personally thank each of my teachers and principals and tell them how much I appreciate their efforts and ask them to forgive me for the many times I could have been a better student.

My classmates gave me a vote of confidence and emphasized that I displayed a very positive attitude because the caption they selected for our yearbook that is printed by my senior picture is: "Success comes in cans, I Can, You Can, We All Can."

Chapter 9:

FORBIDDEN LOVE

❯❮

My four high school years flew by. With work after school and on Saturday I didn't have time for a social life. My social life was still at the Evergreen Baptist Church. The church had programs and events for the young people, so any social activity I participated in was with friends at church from our community. I had no contact with the members of my class other than being with them in classes. I never had a date during my years at LHS. I planned to ask a person for a date to the Senior banquet, but I procrastinated and when I finally asked, she had already accepted a date. So much for my aspirations of romance with this beautiful young lady.

I had managed to arrive at asking this particular city gal to the Senior banquet because we had become good friends. This came about because I was asked to try out for the Senior play. I explained that I worked after school, but because others were involved in after school activities, practice would be held after five. I would be off work at that time and available for practice. I landed the part of school Principal in the play "Time Out For Ginger." Mrs. Bennett was the English and Literature teacher and was the director of the play. Ginger was an aspiring girl baseball enthusiast that insisted on trying out for the school baseball team. Our class was way ahead of its time, since this was before Title 9. Ginger's mother was played by Nancy Bennett, so our roles put us together in the same scenes. At practice, we spent time together saying our lines off stage. Ginger's mother, Nancy, was trying to convince me, the Principal, to let her daughter try out to play baseball with the boys. The Principal of the school would have no part of this. The play had many funny lines and was a big hit. Of course, the audience was our high school friends and families.

Nancy and I remained friends, and later that year she asked if I would like to ride on the LHS Christmas float. She was going to be Mary holding baby Jesus and I would be Joseph. This was an honor for me. The annual Christmas parade was a big deal and drew hundreds of families to our small town for the children to get to see Santa Claus and get some free candy. After the parade, Nancy and I were considered a couple by our fellow classmates. We could be seen having friendly chats if the opportunity came along. We didn't advertise the fact that we had never dated. I did resolve to ask her to the Senior Banquet held each year just prior to graduation. After delaying, I finally got up the confidence to ask her. It was too late. She had already accepted another invitation. I don't know if I was relieved or disappointed. It just happened that the guy that asked her to the banquet was voted most handsome in the Senior class. His special recognition would be in our Yearbook.

It turned out that I was not her date for the banquet, but we ended up together. After the banquet, most everyone headed to "The Bridge." I had never heard of it but went along with the crowd. It was an abandoned bridge that was left when the roadway was rerouted. It was a place that seemed to be isolated and was used for drinking and dancing to the car radio. I rode out to the Bridge with my friend, HO, and his date, Gail. Nancy's handsome date was drinking, and she was afraid for him to take her home. So she joined me in the car with HO and Gail. HO dropped Nancy off at her house and me at my car. I believe that event made a real impact on her opinion of me. She later referenced the event in my Yearbook.

Then, during exam week, Nancy invited me to a swim party at Lake Tiak-O'Khata. The guys and girls there were all from the city, and even though I was their fellow student for twelve years, I didn't feel comfortable in this group. Besides, I was self-conscience because I was very skinny. I weighed only 120 pounds when I finished high school.

The night after graduation, Nancy invited me to a party given by some of the graduates' parents. It was held at the Louisville Country Club. Again, my old inferiority complex kicked in. I was with Nancy's city friends with whom I had had no prior social relations. I had no dancing experience. Nancy showed me some dance moves while I faked my enjoyment as best I could.

Graduation was a most happy, happy time for me. Seemed the entire church family gave me a graduation present. My bed was covered in new socks, shirts, underwear, neck ties, cuff-links and even cash. Mom had always made certain that she gave presents to the graduates in our church family, so they reciprocated.

A week after graduation, I was on a Greyhound bus bound for Fort Jackson, SC., to attend eight weeks of Military Occupation Speciality (MOS) training. My brother, now working full time with the MS National Guard, had lined up this military skills school for me to train as a clerk typist. He knew this was about the best job the Army had to offer. I would be in with regular Army soldiers. This was how National Guard personnel received special skills training. This assignment would enable me to save enough for most of my first year of college expenses at ECJC. I made additional money by pulling kitchen police, KP, for the fellow soldiers that wanted to go on weekend pass. I would also have a job working in the Student Center at ECJC. With my savings in the summer and the student center job I would be able to cover all of my expenses.

I entered the military school with an excellent typing skill. In high school I could type sixty five words a minute with no errors on a manual typewriter. Needless to say, I was about the best typist they had ever seen at Fort Jackson. Only one bad memory, the gnats at Fort Jackson were terrible and plentiful. Buzzing your face as you typed was not enjoyable. However, I was glad to be there during summer rather than winter. In winter, they used coal for heating and everything was covered in black soot. We had exercises early before breakfast every morning. This was my first experience doing organized exercise. I had never participated in sports in school and we did not have gym classes. It was amazing how good I felt after exercise. Regrettably, I did not continue the daily exercise program after my training. We did have gym classes at ECJC. I got quite good at volleyball.

My brother, Carey, his wife Betty and Mother drove to Fort Jackson to pick me up and save me the trip back home on the bus. It was great having that much time with my family telling them all about my experiences during the training. My first time away from home was probably an anxious time for Mother. I know she was thankful that I made it fine without having any problems. Even though it was my first time away from home, I was too busy to get homesick.

After completion of the training at Fort Jackson, I was home for four weeks before classes started at ECJC. This was the first break for me since I started working at the Five and Dime. My cousin Johnny's Mom had bought a new 54 Chevrolet after Uncle Will died. He and I would ride around on weekends and circle the A1 Drive In. This was the only hamburger and shake restaurant available. It was a favorite hangout for the young people, especially those that had cars that they liked to show off by driving around the drive-in over and over. Johnny also liked to shoot pool. He was very good. I was not very good, and besides I did not feel comfortable in the pool hall. It was not a place I would want Mom and Dad to see me.

During these few free days, I kept having thoughts of Nancy. I was thinking I should call her and ask her for a date. At this point we had never dated, even though she had invited and I attended the swim party and the graduation dance. We had gone to both of these separately and returned from them separately, she with her girl friends and I alone since I was not friends with any of the city guys. After pacing the floor and practicing the words I would use to invite her to go to a movie, I called one mid-afternoon and she accepted. This would be my first real date.

My Dad's advice, "Never date a girl that I would not marry," kept haunting me. What was I doing? Whether it was my inferiority complex or just plain common sense, deep down, I knew Nancy and I would never have a life together. Nancy and her family were members of the Louisville Country Club Society and Presbyterians. My family and I were members of the Country Baptist Church Society. We had said our goodbyes after graduation. She was off to Mississippi State College for Women (MSCW), the school for women of society in MS. I was off to the Junior College for the East Central counties of MS. But still, she had become a very special friend and the fact that she had invited me to join her with her circle of friends must mean that she had special feelings for me.

Since she had been so vividly on my mind during these free days, was I in love with, for the lack of a better word, a "forbidden lover?" Since I had never been in love before, I had to find out why my thoughts of her seemed ever present. In the end, I determined that if it was not meant to be, she would decline my invitation to go to a movie with me. Since she accepted, it confirmed that she must also have feelings for me. She too had probably not experienced being in love, so she too was not sure what was going on.

I was frantically preparing for the upcoming date. I had to decide what to wear. I had to wash and wax the 1947 Chevrolet.

Remember, it is 1957 and our used new car back in 1950 is ten years old. I had the old green Chevy cleaned and polished when I arrived at the Bennett's residence. With dread, I walked up on their front porch contemplating my upcoming conversation with her Dad. I have no idea what I said, but he was nice and friendly and made me feel at ease. I'm certain he could tell I was a nervous wreck. We had a couple more dates before we went our separate ways for college.

We exchanged letters during our first semester and dated during Christmas break. While on Christmas break, she invited me to her church service on Sunday night. This was the church where Dad's brother Ovin was the janitor for cleaning their church each week. Once, when Uncle Ovin was sick, Dad and I cleaned it for him. The night Nancy and I were there, only a small group was in attendance. They seemed to all be very close like family, just the same as in our church. They were friendly and told me they appreciated me coming. Again, I was not comfortable with my association with this level of Louisville society considering my own status in the small town where everyone knew each other and where they fit in. I really did not consider it then, but I wondered later if Nancy's family and friends considered that she was being rebellious by dating me. I believe Nancy was always sincere, always kind and considerate, and I was very fortunate to have her as a friend.

Just prior to the end of my first year at ECJC, I received a letter from Bill Walker, the owner of WE Walker Stores, offering me the Assistant Manager position for the store in Forest, MS. I moved to Forest immediately after finishing the school year. This marked the end of my ties to my home town, because I was never there again other than to visit Mom and Dad. I'm not sure if I wrote to Nancy to tell her of my decision to move to Forest and become a retail guru. Our communications ended at this point. Later, I learned that after her Freshman year she transferred from MSCW to Ole Miss.

In October 1960, two years after moving to Forest, my picture appeared in the Winston County Journal announcing that I had attended Artillery OCS at Fort Sill, OK and received my Commission as a Second Lieutenant in the MS National Guard. It also stated that I was enrolled at ECJC for my second year. That year, just prior to Christmas break, I was very surprised to receive a letter from Nancy. We had had no communication for over two years. She was inviting me to attend the Sugar Bowl game in New Orleans on New Year's Day. Her Uncle, a Doctor living in New Orleans, had two fifty yard line tickets for her and her date. Ole Miss was playing the Naval Academy staring Roger Staubach. (Not true - I will explain later.) You cannot imagine the mixed emotions and excitement I experienced upon receiving this letter. Did this mean a renewal of our romance after all this time? Regardless of what it meant for our relationship, I was not about to miss the biggest event of the year for every sports minded Mississippian. I accepted her invitation and immediately began to plan the much anticipated reunion with Nancy and the trip to New Orleans.

I had not been able to save a dime working at Forest. I had bought a car, and with a car payment and living expenses it took all of my fifty dollars a week to live. My only spending money was from the National Guard, which was paid quarterly. I was getting a big raise in the Guard by getting my commission; however, the money from the raise would not be there until the next quarterly pay period. I needed to raise some cash for the big trip. A classmate had asked me about trading his customized 1954 Ford for my 1956 Ford Fairlane, 2 door hardtop. We negotiated a trade with my receiving five hundred dollars. I was not happy with the 54 Ford. It was a straight shift and did not have the comfortable interior that I enjoyed in my 56 Ford. So I traded the 54 Ford for a 56 Oldsmobile, 2 door hardtop, a sporty gas guzzler. This was not one of my smartest decisions. How could I think straight with what was happening to me and the conflicting thoughts I was having about it all. The next major decision I thought I needed to make was what to wear. At this stage of my life all the wardrobe I had was for attending school. I decided I should wear a suit to the game. I'll never forget my agonizing over the selection in Stubbs Department store. I finally selected a drab, brown, light-weight summer material that I came to regret wearing.

When I picked Nancy up, I could tell she was impressed with my big fancy car. She was as beautiful as I remembered. Our trip down was pleasant enough. It felt like we were eloping. I had never done anything like this before. Taking her out of town and spending the night at her Uncle's, whom I had never met, seemed to be almost improper given the fact that Nancy and I had not communicated in over two years. It was New Year's Eve when we arrived in New Orleans in late afternoon, and the parties were in full swing. Right away I knew I was out of my element. She had not mentioned that her Uncle lived in the French Quarter. We finally got parked as close as possible to his apartment. Of course, being in the French Quarter, I locked the car and that was the start of my frustrating weekend. I locked the keys in the car. What a way to impress your girl and her Uncle. Luckily, a policeman came along and easily opened it.

Once we were in the apartment, Nancy introduced me to Dr. Frank Boswell and his wife Jo. After some small talk, we joined the New Year's Eve revelers on Bourbon Street. We seemed to flow with the crowd and had some food at what seemed to be an open house with food and booze. I didn't know what drink to order and ended up with bourbon and coke, which I very much disliked.

The rest of the evening seems like a blur. We walked from party to party of open houses with food and booze. I didn't enjoy the food and finally settled on plain coke. I was out of my comfort zone. I am sure I was not responding as a typical tourist enjoying party time.

I don't remember having breakfast the next morning. Once we were at the game, the summer suit I purchased proved to be no match for the strong cold wind bringing in a cold front. Our seats on the first row at the fifty-yard line provided no bodies as a shield from the wind. The game was a disappointment, as we watched Roger Staubach beat Ole Miss 14 to 7. (Not true - I explain later.) The loss didn't warm me, nor the much anticipated romance with Nancy. The drive home was awfully quiet. I can be down right rude when I am tired, frustrated, disappointed and hungry all at the same time. At least I was finally warm. We stopped in McComb, MS for a burger and coffee.

I don't know the real reason for my depressed mood. Was it because I was completely out of my comfort zone? Or, was it my disappointment from the realization that Nancy and I could never have a happy life together? We had little in common, so the conversation and togetherness just weren't there. I think she also realized it for I don't remember any meaningful conversation we had all the way home. I am afraid I was more or less silent in my thoughts, and I regret to this day not having an honest dialogue with Nancy about my feelings and why I felt we could never be happy together. Instead, I waited until I was back at school and put all my thoughts and feelings in a letter to her. I gave the best explanation I could for why I thought I could never fit into and be happy in her world.

I know I was wrong to not explain my feelings in person. I hope I was nice and not hurtful in my letter. I never had any response or any communication from Nancy again. Later that year, in October, 1961, my marriage to Kathy was announced in the Winston County Journal. A few years later I saw an announcement for Nancy's marriage to Pete Hairston.

Kathy and I met them at our 25th High School Class reunion. We introduced each other to our spouses, and I recall there was little conversation between us. She and Pete have a son and a daughter. One of my classmates told me a few years ago that Pete was Nancy's angel.

Fast forward to March, 2019. After completing this "Forbidden Love" Chapter, I reached out to Nancy for her to review it and make any changes or additions. I am thankful that I did because some of my memories were wrong. I even had the Ole Miss Rebels playing the wrong team and losing instead of winning. So, we decided she should provide her memories of the trip and I am including them in my book. Nancy provided the following highlights from her memory of our trip to the Sugar Bowl in New Orleans in 1961.

Sugar Bowl NOLA 1961

> During my senior year at Ole Miss, the Rebels had a 10-1 season resulting in an invitation to the Sugar Bowl on January 1, 1961. Impulsively, I bought two tickets before I left for Christmas break. I did not know how or with whom I'd get to New Orleans, but I was pretty sure I had a place to stay.
>
> My uncle Frank and wife, Jo, had an apartment in the French Quarter. He was thirteen years older and felt more like an older brother, so I didn't mind imposing on them. In retrospect, that was pretty presumptuous of me. He had graduated from Millsap's, then Tulane Medical School and practiced general medicine a few years in DeKalb, MS where he met Jo. After he specialized in ophthalmology, they settled in New Orleans.
>
> Now, I needed transportation and a date. I was not dating anyone at the time and had not yet met Pete. Two of my dearest and oldest guy friends, Buddy and Jimmy, had plans, so I asked a friend from high school who I had gotten to know our senior year at LHS.

Keith Livingston accepted my invitation and seemed excited. I loved football and anything New Orleans, so why wouldn't he!

We made a point to cross Lake Pontchartrain on the new Causeway bridge although bridges frighten me.

Frank and Jo's apartment was on the down river side of Jackson Square. They occupied the front section with the owner's apartment in the back separated by a courtyard with a fountain all connected by a long hallway. These buildings look like warehouses from the street but are charming on the inside. We had to buzz to get in after parking on the sidewalk for safety's sake.

Jo is a very good cook (I found out later after visiting many times through the years), but I do not remember what or where we ate that night or any other meal.

Since it was New Year's Eve, we decided to venture up to Bourbon Street. The crowd was claustrophobic and scary. A voice yelled "Dr. Boswell", and a man in overalls with a liquor bottle hanging out of his pocket rushed up and starting shaking Frank's hand. Jo leaned over and whispered, "Marcellus, our plumber in DeKalb". He was delighted to see the Boswells and joined us, uninvited, as we strolled through the revelers.

Possibly trying to lose Marcellus, Frank steered us towards the entrance to Pete Fountains's club where his next set was about to begin. The plumber stayed attached even after the doorman confiscated his booze. As we made our way to our corner table someone yelled "Bennett". It was a friend from the "W", and I wondered what she thought: Frank and Keith in suits and Marcellus in overalls.

We settled into our table, ordered our obligatory drinks, and Marcellus started talking. Pete Fountain quit playing his famed clarinet, walked to the mic and said "will the people at the corner table be quiet or leave." I thought my uncle, who was trying to establish a practice in New Orleans, was going to crawl under the table. Since it was New Year's Eve and Bourbon Street, nobody probably noticed.

Later, we headed back to the apartment without the plumber. Keith and I had a ballgame the next day. Ole Miss beat Rice with Jake Gibbs at quarterback and claimed a part of a national championship. The game was low-scoring and not too exciting, but I was glad I was there.

Our ride back to Louisville was uneventful. We did not see each other again until after we were both married and at our first LHS class reunion. I don't think we mentioned this trip.

Nancy Bennett Hairston

After receiving her memories and digesting her perception of our relationship, I decided I needed to include as part of my memories the acknowledgment that I must have let my ego and imagination run wild regarding our relationship. How could I have considered that I stood a chance of actually being a romantic contender in Nancy's world. I feel privileged to be in the ranking with her group of guy friends.

When you are young, first, it is difficult to know your true feelings and, second, it is hard to be brave enough to communicate them. In our case, the old cliché, "what we have is a failure to communicate," seems appropriate. Having had exposure to a true love experience with Sue Ellen when I worked in Forest, MS, I realized, after the trip to New Orleans, that Nancy and I had never had that. If only I had been brave enough to communicate, there would never have been a letter to break off a friendship. Even though I cannot remember what I said in the letter, I now regret the letter even more and apologize for whatever I said.

I have some additional advice for my grandchildren: "Be careful if you date your friend, it could ruin a beautiful friendship."

My memory of the Sugar Bowl game makes for a funny story. I had told people for years that I saw Roger Staubach beat Ole Miss in the Sugar Bowl game in 1961. Not true. As Nancy pointed out, Ole Miss Quarterback, Jake Gibbs, beat Rice in the 1961 Sugar Bowl game that we saw together. Navy played Ole Miss in the Sugar Bowl in 1955. George Welch was the Navy Quarterback not Roger Staubach. I was not there. Evidently, I suffer from SELECTIVE or WISHFUL memory. So don't take my book as totally factual!

Chapter 10:

EAST CENTRAL JUNIOR COLLEGE

I am not proud of my first year at East Central Junior College (ECJC). I guess I was sowing my wild oats. I know I continued to stray further from a life serving my Savior. At Fort Jackson I had the opportunity to attend chapel every Sunday, but instead I pulled KP for the guys that wanted to leave post for the weekend. I went to the service only once. It was a very small group in attendance. At East Central, rather than attend the Baptist Church across the street from the campus I would sleep in on Sunday. I did not join the Baptist Student Union (BSU) which was the best way to meet other Christians on campus.

My dorm was Winston Hall, a barracks type long open area with cots every few feet. There were about thirty on our second floor. We all shared a large shower with a row of commodes. Not much privacy to say the least. At night there were card games and music on radios. Not very productive for study. I did most of my studying at the library. The guys near me in the dorm were from Louisville. I fell in with this group, but should have joined the BSU.

All of us were taking business courses. Accounting under Mr. Bedwell was really difficult. He had a way of getting you very confused between what was a debit or credit. Someone came up with the idea to steal Mr. Bedwell's exam. They went into Bedwell's office through a window and sure enough located the exam with answers. They copied down the question number and recorded the answer. This took some time, but it was in the middle of the night and no one was up. There was no night watchman for the campus or campus police. Several of us stood watch to make sure no one was about to discover us. We made sure we did not get every question correct and to vary the ones we got wrong. Still, Mr. Bedwell was shocked at how well everyone did. We had shared the answers with several others in the class. I think practically all in the class had the answers.

This was the worst thing I had ever done. Had we been caught, we would have been sent home. How could I have participated in something that had the potential to bring shame on my family and betray my Christian faith. I was proof that when you are young, your judgment is overruled by your desire to fit in and be accepted. My low esteem and feelings of inferiority contributed to my going along with the crowd.

The exam theft was not my only action that would have resulted in my dismissal if I had been caught. One afternoon when I was free from classes, the same group of buddies invited me to go with them to the beer joint just over the line into Lauderdale county. At that time Mississippi was a dry state, but some counties had beer joints and bootleggers that paid off the sheriff. It was common knowledge that the sheriff of Lauderdale County made more money than the President of the United States. I let them know that I had never tasted a beer. This was a mistake because when we got there, they insisted on buying me a beer, then another. I think I had three beers and had nothing to eat. I was totally drunk. When we headed home, I was feeling no pain, happy as a clown. Then it hit me. They had to stop and let me vomit on the side of the highway. After that I passed out. I did not remember anything until I awoke the next morning, still in my clothes, feeling terrible. They said they had carried me up the stairs and dropped me on my cot and that I never moved. Thankfully, it was dark when we got back and no one in authority saw my condition. Had I been discovered drunk, I would have been sent home in shame.

For weeks I felt guilty and embarrassed around campus, for I knew word about me got around to everyone, probably even some of the teachers. One good thing resulted in my introduction to beer, I never drank another one for many years. I never acquired a taste for beer the rest of my life. The same thing happened to me with wine. While I was working in Forest, I had some wine for the first time. I got very sick and never drank any more wine. I still do not care much for wine. I only wish that cigarettes had made me sick the first time I inhaled. My brother got very sick on his first ciga-rette, and he never smoked all of his life.

I did not date anyone my first year at ECJC. Nancy and I wrote a few letters and we dated on Christmas break. I never took her to my church or to meet my Mom and Dad. I guess I considered her my girl but we both avoided the committing phrase of "I Love You."

I made good grades at ECJC because I studied. I even helped Shurden, a friend from Louisville, with his accounting studies. He went home every weekend because he was dating a girl that was still in high school. When I didn't have student center duty, I would ride with him. He lived only two miles from my house, so it was not inconvenient for him to drop me at my house. He had a brand new 1957 red Ford convertible. Mom worried about me riding with him. Once, when driving drunk late at night, he had failed to stop and turn left or right at a dead-end street. Instead, he plowed straight into a house. Thankfully there were no injuries. The accident was in the weekly paper, the Winston County Journal, so everyone, including my Mother, knew about his drinking. I went to work for WE Walker stores and did not return for my second year at ECJC. Shurden was upset that I was not returning. He also did not return and instead worked in his Dad's timber and sawmill operation. Shurden committed suicide when he was in his forties. I regret that I was such a poor Christian witness to Shurden. He seemed to respect me and would have been receptive. I could have made a difference in his life. He did not have many friends.

The letter I received from Bill Walker offering me the Assistant Manager's job at the Five and Dime in Forest, MS was part of God's plan for my life, because when I returned to ECJC two years later, I would meet my love and lifelong partner.

Chapter 11:

A FIVE AND DIME CAREER

><|<

M y move to Forest, MS, immediately after school ended, went smoothly. Mom and Dad delivered me and my few belongings. Saying goodbye was rather emotional for both them and myself. I would know no one. With no car, I was confined to my apartment and store where I worked. I would not be able to visit Mom and Dad until I got a car. I would only have Sundays off and it would not be worth it to ride a bus to Louisville and back the same day. There was probably no bus service anyway that would make the round trip in one day.

Mr. Thompson, the VP for the bank next door to the Five and Dime, had a room in his house that he rented. Only problem, the room already had an occupant, a teller that worked in the bank, Joe Majors. The room had a chest of drawers and a small closet but was ample for my limited wardrobe. There were two single beds and Joe's TV stationed on the chest. We shared a bathroom across the hall.

The months before I was able to buy a car were rather boring. I walked the two blocks to the store and stopped in the cafe that was one block from the store for my three meals a day. This was convenient, but after buying a car with a hefty car payment, I discovered

I could not afford this menu on my fifty dollars per week. Joe and I watched TV most every night or read. Joe was a bachelor about thirty years old. He had a bum leg as a result of polio. He was content to watch TV and read. He had a very friendly personality, and everyone in town liked him. He had lived in Forest a few years and was a loyal fan and attended all the sports events at the High School.

Work at the Five and Dime was very routine. I had three middle age ladies that worked full time and two that came in on Saturdays. My boss, Mr. Ethel Boyles, the manager of the store, was also a district manager that checked on other stores in the chain. Each week he would travel to one of them and evaluate their operation and determine if they had any problems that needed his attention. I was acting manager in his absence. All of the ladies knew their jobs, for they had worked for several years at the store. None were ever a problem. Anyone of them could have done my job probably better, but this was before women were assigned as managers. Each of the ladies had an assigned section of the store for tracking inventory and reordering merchandise as needed. This was before computer data processing inventory control. Everything we did was with paper and pencil. Their major responsibility was to help each individual customer in a friendly manner and encourage the customer to buy and return again. They were the sales force for the store.

My major daily responsibility other than opening and closing was to count the cash for the two cash registers. There were no credit cards used. It was all cash transactions. I always counted the cash with at least one of the ladies as witness. The bank deposit slip was always completed after the cash was counted. The total of each denomination of change and bills was listed. Then the total for the deposit was entered into a ledger that contained the sales for each day of the week. This was completed in duplicate. All of this was placed in the safe in the stockroom. The deposit was made the next morning when the bank opened. The stamped deposit slip was then put with the weekly ledger sheet and the weekly ledger sheet with deposit slips were mailed on Saturday night after closing to the home office in Columbia, MS. This was the manual accounting process before the introduction of data processing.

Another major task for me was accepting the many parcels that were delivered by the Post Office for the orders that we had placed. I inspected the contents for accuracy and determined if there were any damages. Then I would add the shipping cost to the invoice and calculate the cost per item. Then, using a prepared markup table, I would price the articles. Most of our merchandise had a 50% to 75% markup. A few items would have a 100% markup. These were special order items that we might later put on sale if they did not sell well. The routine items that sold over and over were usually marked up 50%.

Gradually I got to know some of the guys that worked at some of the other stores. One, Jimmy McGee, and I became good friends. He worked at the department store across the street. We had coffee and lunch together. He was a fun guy never serious about anything, which went well with my always being very serious. He already had a car, so at last I could do something other than watch TV with Joe.

Like Louisville, Forest had a drive-in burger joint where the young people circled and showed off their fancy or not so fancy cars. When I finally was able to buy a car, I bought a used '56 Ford Fairlane, two door hard-top with glass pack mufflers. It was very sharp, and with the loud glass packs I felt like I had finally arrived. Loud mufflers were a fad at the time, as well as drag racing. I never once was tempted to drag race, although I was challenged a few times. But, I simply replied that I did not drag.

Jimmy and I were always trying to make friends with the local girls, but they were all still in High School and we were never successful. Our age group was all away at college or had moved to Jackson or Meridian to find jobs. Then Jimmy had the great idea to go to Jackson or Meridian to see if we could find a date. So, one

Sunday night we headed to Meridian, forty five miles east of Forest on famous Highway Eighty. We drove up to a burger drive-in and parked. This was not a circle drive-in. We were only there a few minutes when a car with two young ladies pulled in beside us. We were in my car and Jimmy was in the passenger seat. Of course he immediately rolled down the window and started up a conversation with the ladies. Jimmy was not the least bit bashful and never met a stranger. In ten minutes, Jimmy gets out of the car and has one of the girls in the back seat with him and the other was in the front seat with me. This was the beginning of my second experience with that thing called love.

After buying a car with a hefty car payment, I could no longer afford to eat three meals a day at the convenient cafe. I searched around and found a two room apartment, bedroom and kitchen, with a roommate to share expenses. This was ideal. Now, with a kitchen my expenses would be much less, and the rent was the same as at the VP's house. My roommate this time was also in his early thirties. We alternated cooking supper each night. I would prepare spaghetti with hamburger meat and he would broil a steak and bake a potato. The small apartment was near the store, so I could come home at lunch and have a sandwich. Breakfast was a doughnut and coffee at the cafe with Jimmy.

At this time, my expenses were breaking even with my income, even with a weekly trip to Meridian, dating my new girlfriend. This set up was short lived, for my engaged roommate was getting married and moving out. I could not afford to handle the apartment rent alone, so again I was looking to find a home that I could afford. I immediately found this room for rent with kitchen privileges. It was a beautiful old antebellum home owned by a widowed, retired school teacher named Mrs. McLaughlin. It was located in a well maintained, older neighborhood across the street from her brother's home which was also large and well maintained. He was the Circuit Judge for the counties around Forest. Mrs. McLaughlin had two daughters that lived in Arizona. They came for a visit once a year, and Mrs. McLaughlin went out to Arizona to visit them once a year. This place was a wonderful place to live. I had a private large bedroom with an adjoining private bathroom. Often, Mrs. McLaughlin would invite me to have supper with her if I was home when she was having her meal. Being able to use the kitchen solved my expense for meals. This was where I lived the remaining time I lived in Forest.

Two events are seared into my memory that occurred in the old house. One would have taken my life, in my opinion, had God not decided it was not my time to go. The bathroom had an overhead light, and also a light by the mirror with a metal pull chain. Being a penny pincher, I always pulled the chain to turn the light off after I finished shaving but before I stepped into the bathtub. This one night I failed to turn off the light by the mirror until I was showering and noticed the light was still on. The tub drain was slow, so about an inch of water had accumulated in the tub from the shower. When I pulled the metal chain, the water and I flew out of the tub. I was semi-conscious for a minute. For many prayers after that, I was thanking God for sparing my life. I don't mess with electricity in the bathroom anymore.

Another event that was very strange happened one night that had never happened before and has never happened since. It had to have been a dream. If not, there was definitely a ghost that walked around in my room when I was sleeping. I felt wide awake as I listened to these footsteps walking in my room. I could not decide if I should get up and turn the light on and confront the person or not. I just lay there and eventually the walking stopped. Then I got up and turned the light on and searched the rooms near mine, but of course there was no one. This happened when Mrs. McLaughlin was away on her trip to Arizona. Whichever it was, dream or ghost, I know it had something to do with the house, because it has never happened anywhere else the rest of my life.

During this time, I would travel to Meridian once a week for a date with Sue Ellen. This put stress on my fifty dollars weekly income to pay for gas, movies, and eating shakes and burgers. I did receive a fifty dollar Christmas bonus but no raise. My pride would not allow me to ask for a raise, or it could have been that my self-confidence was weak. My National Guard pay each quarter provided extra income, for I had been promoted to the rank of Specialist Five.

When I moved to Forest, I transferred from the National Guard Unit in Decatur to Bravo Battery in Forest commanded by Captain Jessie Blaylock. He and I clicked right away. With the clerk typist school on my record, he assigned me as the Battery Company Clerk working directly for the full-time technician, Master Sergeant McNeal. Often, he used me to help him with paperwork to prepare for various inspections. This gave me extra drill time and additional pay for my quarterly paycheck.

One drill night in early April, 1960, Captain Blaylock told me about an opportunity for our unit to send someone to Artillery Officer Candidate School (OCS) at Fort Sill, OK. He explained that it would be ninety days of very difficult physical, mental and academic training. Upon satisfactory completion, I would be commissioned a Second Lieutenant in the MS National Guard. If I was interested, I would have to be approved by Colonel Walker, the BN Commander, and the Group Commander, General Ferguson. General Ferguson was the current President of ECJC and knew me when I was a Freshman. I would also need to pass a physical exam. I told Captain Blaylock that I was definitely interested. The paperwork was started, and a physical was scheduled with a local Doctor in Forest. The approvals came through highly recommending me based on my record for the four years that I had now been in the MS National Guard. The ninety day training started on June 1 and ended on August 29, 1960. This meant that I would need a three month leave of absence from the Five and Dime.

I began to evaluate my retail career and I believe God gave me some very good reasons that I should take this opportunity to go back to college and get my degree in order to advance my career opportunities. My retail career was providing the bare necessities and I decided I should and could do better. If I received my commission, my National Guard earnings plus a job at school would be enough to cover my expenses. OCS ended in time for me to be at ECJC for my second year without missing any classes. I made the decision to resign from the Assistant Manager Position just prior to finishing my second year. It had been a short career, but in many respects, it seemed a long time. I gave two weeks notice on the tenth of May. This gave me one week to be at home in Louisville to prepare myself physically and build my self-confidence.

Everyone at the store and the friends I had made in Forest were excited for me and congratulated me on deciding to return to college. All wished for my success. Even Mr. Boyles did not try to talk me out of my new plan. He also did not mention a raise. One of the ladies had everyone over to her home, and they gave me a sendoff dinner.

I believe my short retail career was successful. I did a good job and the folks admired my dependability and hard work. I came in with a learning attitude and treated them with respect. I don't regret the two years at Forest. In fact, it resulted in my long career as an officer in the Army National Guard and Reserves that would not have happened had I never become associated with Captain Blaylock.

My decision to resign and return to ECJC after completion of OCS was a critical turning point in my life. It resulted in many more unbelievably successful life Chapters. Even though during those two years I was not growing my relationship with Christ, God was still believing in me and directing His plan for my life beyond anything I could possibly have imagined.

On the way to Mom and Dad's from Forest I stopped in to see Mrs. Cross, the Manager of the Student Center where I had worked my Freshman year at ECJC. I wanted to find out if she could help me with a job for the coming fall semester. She was delighted that I planned to return to college and excited for me that I had the opportunity to go to OCS. She explained that since I now had a car and could go to the Post Office in town to pick up the college mail, she wanted me to be the school postman and run the post office. This was the most prestigious job on campus and paid almost all of my college expenses.

Chapter 12:

DID THE NATIONAL GUARD SAVE ME FROM MARRIAGE?

▰

The two ladies we met at the Meridian drive-in were friendly, and like Jimmy and me, they were interested in meeting someone. They were our age, had finished high school in 1957, and were working. Sue Ellen Pratt was the name of the girl that got into the front seat with me. In my opinion, she was very good looking. We seemed to immediately strike up a conversation. She was easy to talk to and even laughed at my attempts to be funny bantering back and forth with Jimmy about our conquest to find a girl. She worked in a jewelry store. She attended the First Baptist Church of Meridian and claimed to have done clothes modeling for Sears catalog. I had never thought about models for a catalog, but I assumed that it meant she was good looking. Things moved along fast and within an hour Jimmy and I had both made dates with them for the following Saturday night. We double dated for that first date. But for the second date we did not plan a double date. Jimmy decided he did not like his date, so after the second date he never returned to Meridian, mainly because at this time he met June, a nurse in Forest. They were a perfect couple. They were later married. Sue Ellen and I double dated with Jimmy and June on several occasions.

Sue Ellen was everything that Nancy was not. She was a city girl but not in society. She was raised by her Grandmother because her Mother left home and went to New York and basically abandoned her family. She only knew her Mother from pictures and stories told to her by her Grandmother and Dad. I never met her Dad. He supposedly was working and living with relatives in Texas. Once Sue Ellen went out to visit him for a few days. She and her Grandmother lived in this huge old house in an old section of Meridian. I met her Grandmother. She was very old but very alert and easy to talk with. I could tell she loved Sue Ellen dearly. I also met a favorite Aunt and her family. Sue Ellen was very close to this family, and Sue Ellen seemed to be their favorite relative.

I fell into a weekly routine of driving to Meridian on Sunday afternoon for a date with Sue Ellen. We went to movies or bowling and had burgers and shakes. We enjoyed each others' company and could talk about everything. Before I knew it, I was planning a trip to introduce her to my folks, something I would not have dreamed of doing for Nancy. I would have been too embarrassed for Nancy to see our humble dwelling, but I was very comfortable for Sue Ellen to see it. This was the only time I had ever brought a girl home to meet Mom and Dad. They were very comfortable with Sue Ellen and liked her very much. She had this warm personality and humbleness about her. We went to Evergreen church on Sunday with Mom and Dad. It felt great showing off my good looking girlfriend to my church family.

It was raining hard on our way back from visiting Mom and Dad. It was difficult to see good on the narrow dark highway between Philadelphia and Meridian. I met a car and for a second was blinded by their bright lights, so I hit the brakes. When I did the car spun around and backed off the highway onto a dirt apron. After sitting there a few minutes to catch my breath and recover, I looked, and that apron was the only strip of dirt that I could see. Had the car not landed on this small island of dirt we would have gone into a water filled bog. I believe God had reached out and guided the car onto the only safe spot available.

Another very serious event occurred while on a double date with Jimmy and June. I had brought Sue Ellen to Forest to show her the Five and Dime where I worked and the house where I lived. Jimmy and June joined us, and when we were taking Sue Ellen back to Meridian, Jimmy asked if he could drive. He was so tall he didn't fit well in the back seat. So, Sue Ellen and I were in the back seat. On the way, Sue Ellen went to sleep, or so I thought. It was winter and the heater was on. It was stuffy, and I got sleepy. Thankfully, I opened my window just a small crack. When we arrived in Meridian, we could not wake Sue Ellen. June suspected immediately that it could be carbon monoxide poisoning. We immediately opened windows, and Jimmy headed for the nearest hospital emergency entrance. When we arrived, Sue Ellen was barely breathing. They treated her in the ER for about two hours before they were certain that she would be OK. She had extreme headaches for several days afterward. My desirable glass pack mufflers were leaking, and I vowed to get rid of them. I had nightmares about this near-death experience that my car had caused for Sue Ellen.

I knew Sue Ellen was anxious to get married, because she confided in me that she was occasionally dating a guy in Meridian. This seemed to be her hinting that I needed to get serious about marriage, which we had never discussed. I do know we felt like we loved each other and enjoyed everything we did together. It was the first time I felt for sure that I was in love. I believe I was very close to proposing to Sue Ellen, but God had other plans for our lives. Captain Blaylock presented the opportunity for me to attend OCS and become a commissioned officer in the MS National Guard. This pushed any thoughts about marriage to the back of my mind, because I began to see a way for me to finish my second year at ECJC and maybe continue my education and get my degree.

As soon as the official approvals came through for me to attend OCS, I gave my notice to my boss at the Five and Dime. I made a date to tell Sue Ellen of my future plans. It was not easy for me. I actually cried. I suspected that I was telling her goodbye. I knew as a student I would not be able to afford to drive to Meridian for dates. She took my explanation of my new plans very well. She was very understanding and did not discourage me or try to change my mind. I wondered later if she was more disappointed than she was willing to show. We agreed to write while I was at OCS, if and when I had the time. We exchanged a few letters, but I could tell from them that she was moving on and was not expecting that one day I would come around and propose marriage. She realized I had other priorities that did not include her. We had one more date for old times' sake. I called her and persuaded her to attend a football game at ECJC. I had the opportunity to show off my beautiful ex-girlfriend to my buddies. That was the end of our relationship and any conversations.

Years later, when I was the IBM Administration Manager in Jackson, MS, a hospital in Meridian was refusing to pay their IBM invoices due to a disagreement with the salesman. I sent the sales representative to visit their Accounts Payable department. He came back and told me a lady working in Accounts Payable said to tell me hello. Her name was Sue Ellen. I called her and we talked. I made an Accounts Receivable call to clear up the accounting issues and get the invoices paid. I also had coffee with Sue Ellen in the break room. She was happily married, and we shared pictures of our children, her beautiful daughter and my two boys. She said after she had gall bladder surgery, she gained too much weight. She must have weighed almost 200 pounds. She was still sweet, and her face was still beautiful. However, I am thankful that the National Guard had probably saved me from marrying Sue Ellen. God had a better plan for me.

Chapter 13:

OFFICER CANDIDATE SCHOOL - OCS CLASS R60

U pon arrival at Mom and Dad's for my week of getting psyched for the biggest challenge of my young life, I concentrated on getting myself into the best possible physical condition. I knew I could not do it in one week, but my goal was to improve enough to pass the physical test administered early at the start of OCS. They did the test early to flunk out those that could not pass. I jogged, did push-ups, chin-ups and sit-ups. I knew all of these were on the test. My arm strength had always been good, and because my body weight was so light, I felt confident I would do well. Having never done timed runs, I had no idea how long it would take me to run the mile which had to be run in ten minutes. I ran every day until I could do a mile in ten minutes. I did more exercise that week than I had ever done or done since. My physical condition was improved. I had more confidence which I needed badly.

A list was provided of all the uniforms we needed to bring. My unit pulled out the newest they had in their inventory. The first day at OCS we took all our uniforms to a laundry. They tailor fitted us so the uniforms fit us like a glove, leaving no chance for a wrinkle anywhere on them.

I caught a ride to Fort Sill with another candidate from our Artillery Group, Patrick Thornton. Patrick flunked the physical and was sent home. So much for my ride home. Maybe my brother could come pick me up.

When we arrived at Fort Sill, we ambled into the orderly room in our civilian clothes. They had not told us to wear our uniforms. We found out immediately we had to have our uniforms on in order to report in. This was the initial harassment, for they made us go to the restroom and change into a uniform. Of course, it was wrinkled from being in a duffel bag, which we were told was all we could bring. It had to hold everything that we brought, no suitcases. After we were in uniform, we reported in and were told anytime we were outside we had to run. We literally hit the ground running.

Just as I made it to the famous Robinson Barracks, but before I could step inside, a Redbird caught me. A Redbird was a regular Army, not reserve, soldier that had successfully completed 90 days of OCS and was allowed to harass us anywhere they caught us, except inside the barracks and inside the classroom. They wore a red felt cloth tab on their shoulder, thus the name Redbird. They could harass us in the mess hall. This particular Redbird had a very strong German accent. Foreign countries also used Fort Sill to train their Artillery Officers. He screamed inches from my face for what seemed like an hour with such stuff as "You look like a sick puke miserable jerk." I had to always scream back, "Yes sir," no matter what he said. He asked if I had a girlfriend. When I screamed, "Yes sir," then he started in on her and how horrible she must look and how stupid she must be. It finally ended by him having me do twenty push-ups. That was a traumatic experience. It took me some thirty minutes after I got inside the barracks to recover. It actually scared me, and I wondered if I had to endure this every day. It turned out this was the first and only time I got harassed outside. I always kept a sharp eye and if I spotted a Redbird, I darted inside a building as fast as I could. This experience was my introduction to OCS before I even got into the barracks, my home for the next ninety days.

There were two to four candidates from each state that had Artillery units in the National Guard or Reserves. This special OCS class was conducted each year to keep a fresh supply of officers trained in the latest warfare doctrine for artillery. Each barracks held thirty candidates. We each had a cot, foot locker and metal cabinet that was just wide enough to hold our hanging uniforms. All of these were inspected every morning, plus our boots and shoes for any dust, wrinkles on the bed, any wrinkled uniform or any item in the footlocker that was out of place or dusty. These inspections produced demerits, which produced hours of marching on the parking lot on Sundays. I was very, very fortunate having to march only two hours during my entire tour.. Some had to march the full four hours every Sunday, which was the maximum demerits for one week. This was during the hottest months of summer and was no fun. It also cut into the important study time.

Within hours of arriving, we were told we were going to the Post Exchange (PX), to buy the items that we must display in our foot-locker, precisely the way the picture diagram showed. Of course, we had to run to the PX. On the way we crossed an open field with a ditch that you jumped. When I jumped, I sprained both my ankles. It didn't seem that bad, so I kept going. That night my ankles were swollen. So, after lights were out at 11 pm, as I was soaking my ankles with rubbing alcohol, our barracks officer came through to check that everyone was in bed. He caught me and ordered me to report to sick call the next morning. I knew this would be the end of my OCS. I did some strong praying and pleading for God to heal me and let me finish OCS. Sick call was not where I needed to be. Missing a class or the review for a quiz could really make it difficult to make the grade. The nurse that checked my ankles said I could not afford to miss class. He thought I had come on my own and was just goofing off, as sometimes happens. That is when I told him my barracks officer ordered me to go to sick call. He gave me a slip authorizing me to walk instead of run. So I walked for two days when my unit was running in formation to class. I never missed any class time. My ankles got better. I was embarrassed to be walking and my unit running. I was lucky no one gave me a hard time about it.

All of our classes except the field exercises were held in the appropriately named Snow Hall. It was kept cold enough to snow. This was to keep us awake. We only got six hours sleep each night, 11 to 5. If anyone nodded off in class, a ball was thrown at them with the intent to hit them.

We were kept busy back in the barracks with little harassment rules. We had to file all our brass down so that it was flat. This took a long time. All brass had to be shinned every night, as were boots and shoes. If everything was not perfect, the demerits would be issued. Studies took any spare time we had. The very worst harassment was in the mess hall. A Redbird sat at the head of every table. They would not allow us to move our head up, down or sideways. Looking straight ahead, we had to eat by forking food, then bring it out and up and back to our mouth, still looking straight ahead. If the Redbird caught you looking down at your plate, he would single you out with some smart remark. This went on for about two weeks, but we gradually learned we could move our eyes slightly to see down and do better at getting enough food to survive. Our real solution was as soon as it got dark, a vendor would arrive at the window of our barracks and sell us pizza and burgers. I was starved and bought extra food each night. I actually gained weight, my heaviest ever at 155 pounds when I finished OCS.

Thankfully the physical test was conducted at the end of the second week. My ankles had completely healed. I had no problem passing all of the required minimum repetitions, exceeding most all of them. My mile run was average. My total score even surprised me. I know my week of training helped me do well. This gave me confidence and the desire to try very hard in every class so that I would be a strong performer at OCS. I'm not sure I had ever thought about doing my very best before this, but I was motivated to do just that. We were all competing with each other, yet we were supporting and encouraging each other. We had developed artillery "esprit de corps."

It gets very hot in OK in the summer. When the wet bulb reached 100°, we did not have to run. Also, if 100° and classes ended early, we were marched to the swimming pool for an hour of swimming. We were required to stand under a shower of very cold water for 30 seconds before we could hit the pool. I could barely stand this. Ever since then, I cannot stand cold water on my body. Most all pools are not warm enough for me, and I cannot enjoy the ocean anywhere that I have tried the water. It must be that I have so little fat that the cold goes straight to my bones.

The only night that I drew guard duty, I had an encounter with the Post Military Police. I was guard for our barracks, walking back and forth between the two buildings about the length of a football field. It was after midnight when an MP Jeep drove into our area with blue lights blinking and stopped near me. The two MP's got out and asked me to show my hands. I could not imagine what was going on. They asked if I had seen anyone in the area. When I told them no, I had not, they explained that a rape had taken place and the assailant was on foot in this area. They told me to be on the lookout for a person out alone at this time of night, and if I saw anyone to call the MP number using the barracks phone. Thankfully, nothing further happened that night and I never heard anything about it.

We always got our mail at noon. Once we were on our way to the field, riding in the back of a two and half ton truck, when I got a real upsetting letter. My Dad had emergency surgery for appendicitis. He was doing well. They had not told me when it happened because they did not want me to worry. I was thankful to God that Dad was well.

We all had to perform a minimum of one leadership assignment. I had been platoon leader and also flag bearer in marching formation. My most important leadership assignment was battery commander. I assembled the OCS class in the morning, took roll call from the platoon leaders, then reported the results to the school commandant. You were graded on voice and accuracy of commands and display of confidence. I was nervous, but I scored well.

The artillery training was both classroom and on the job in the field. It was divided into three functions. The Firing Battery was the operations at the guns. We learned and performed each responsibility of the two-man gun crew. I had done this on our two week summer camp training, so I did well in class and performing on the gun.

The Forward Observer was the second function. This was also a two-man team, an officer and a radio operator. They maneuvered themselves as near the enemy position as possible in order to call and adjust artillery rounds onto targets that could be seen with binoculars. I was not familiar with this activity, but I did well in the classroom work and in the live exercises in the field. One day I did a perfect exercise of adjusting the rounds, first above the target, then below, then on the target, before calling for fire for effect. The range officer said, "Gentlemen, that is the way it is done." That was a huge compliment. My score for Forward Observer was great. I'm not sure that was very smart of me, since the Forward Observer assignment is the most dangerous one of all the jobs in Artillery.

The Fire Direction Center (FDC) was the final operation, and it was always staffed by officers assigned to Battalion (BN) Headquarters. They were the best educated personnel in the unit. They had to use advanced math and trig to convert the directions sent by the Forward Observer into an azimuth, elevation and number of powder bags, then send that information to the gun crew.

Wooden slide rules were used along with fixed tables to arrive at the critical information for use by the gun crew. Computers are used today for this operation, but in my day it was all manual. The least miscalculation could put a round into your own unit's location. A few rounds in our training at Camp Shelby, MS put rounds into a chicken house. The chicken farmer claimed he had thousands of chickens in that house. Naturally, the government had to pay for them. Both the classroom work and the field exercise for FDC were very difficult for me. I had no previous experience, so it was all new. When the final graduation scores were posted, I was one happy candidate. I received a 70 in FDC which meant I would graduate.

We had to pass each of the three major Artillery functions. Failure in any one of them meant that you did not graduate. However, the Adjutant General's Office in your home state had the option to award your commission after you completed Artillery School courses at home in the functions that you did not pass. It was a great relief and proud moment to know that I would be receiving my commission when I returned to MS.

Our final weekend, we all got a pass to go into the town of Lawton, OK to celebrate. This was the first and only time we were allowed off post. Some of us in my barracks rented a room at a nice hotel. Most of them were having drinks to celebrate. I had very little because I remembered my experience with beer my first year at ECJC when I got very sick and passed out. I spent most of my weekend some extra sleep on a nice bed instead of a hard, narrow army cot.

The following Monday was spent accounting for and turning in our equipment, and more importantly, getting paid. That was the most cash I had ever had in my life. Then we practiced our graduation to be held the next morning. At noon, we were treated with a very special lunch that featured steak and shrimp. The shrimp poisoned several of us, I am not sure how many. I passed out and do not remember anything that had happened. I awoke on my cot in the barracks, feeling that I had just had the best sleep I had ever had. I was told that we were rushed to the hospital in an ambulance. They pumped out our stomachs and delivered us back to the barracks. They must have also given us a strong sedative. I felt no pain from any of the event. After learning what had happened, I again thanked God for my life being spared. This was at least four times now that I believe God had a hand in allowing me to live.

The next day I felt fine and graduated. It was both a joyful and sad time. We had grown close as a group striving together, sharing the hard times and good times. We knew we would be going to our different states and would probably never see each other again. After I retired, some 45 years later, I got a list of all the guys in my class and tried to locate some of them. I found only one down in Florida. When I talked to him, he didn't remember me. I could not even find the guy that gave me a ride home. I had posted a need for a ride to MS on the bulletin board. Candidate Robert E. Lee from Rome, GA, said I could ride with him if I would help him drive. He planned to drive non-stop passing through MS. I explained it would detour him about sixty miles out of his way to drop me in Louisville, MS. He insisted he didn't mind if I shared the gas and the driving. So, we left at noon and drove all night, arriving at Mom and Dad's early in the morning. Mom fixed us a big country breakfast. We invited him to stay over and rest up, but no, he was on his way to Rome, GA. He was married and anxious to get home to be with his family. I regret that I did not correspond and keep a friendship with Robert E. Lee of Rome, GA.

My completing and graduating from Artillery OCS was a turning point in my life. Next to graduating from high school, it meant more to me than anything I had experienced. I had a new self-confidence, and a greater ambition for my life. My inferiority complex was on life support. I now had to be careful not to act superior to others, especially the enlisted personnel in my guard unit. The example set by the Redbirds at OCS was burned into my memory but was not the example I should follow. I had previously considered myself humble like my Dad. I think that characteristic fit me better than displaying an air of superiority. Prior to OCS, I had not made any plans to stay in the Guard for the rest of my life. Now that I was an officer, with proper assignments and promotions, I could remain in the National Guard or Army Reserves for twenty eight years as an officer. That became my new goal.

Chapter 14:

MY MILITARY CAREER

⊰⊱

After receiving my Commission as a Second Lieutenant in the Mississippi National Guard, I was assigned as Ammunition Officer for Service Battery at Decatur, home of ECJC. My new commander was Captain Denver Brackeen. He was an outstanding basketball player at Ole MS and was named to the All-American team. He even played in the pros for a short time. He was a pleasure to know and work for. He placed full confidence in me and never questioned any decisions I made as commander of my small unit of enlisted men. We hauled ammunition from the Ammo Dump to the gun positions. We had to know where the guns were located, and we had to have the munitions there on time and in the correct quantity. We never failed. I got in there and worked side by side with my men. They respected me for that. It was dangerous duty, but we had safety rules that we followed almost all the time. I was promoted to First Lieutenant while in this assignment.

I left Service Battery and the MS National Guard when I was hired by IBM in Little Rock, Arkansas. There I transferred to a Signal Company in the Arkansas National Guard. I knew nothing about signal. We provided equipment that allowed the different organizations in a battle area to communicate. The equipment at that time was huge and complicated to operate. Most of the antennas we used required line of sight, which required us to locate on the highest point possible in the battle area. I never learned much about signal. We lived only two years in Little Rock before moving to Jackson, MS, at which time I rejoined the Artillery BN in the MS National Guard. It is amazing to think back on how huge and complicated the operation of the military signal equipment was, and today much more capability is in the palm of your hand, Smart-phone.

Since I was the rookie in the Signal Unit, I drew the assignments no one else wanted. On our two week summer camp, we had to convoy to Fort Hood, TX, the closest post to Little Rock large enough for us to utilize the Signal equipment in a real size battle area. I led an advance detachment to get to the bivouac area in time to have the cooks prepare a hot meal for the main convoy. We had to bivouac one night because it was a two day trip. Going went fine, but the return trip did not go well. We all went without enough sleep because we had to leave at 3 am. One of the vehicles crashed into the one in front when we stopped at a stop light. One guy hurt his leg and one of the trucks had some damage. This required an investigation and Survey Report for the injury and damage to government property. This was not appreciated by the office technicians that had to deal with the paperwork.

After two years with IBM in Little Rock, I attended an IBM meeting in New Orleans for training. The Administrator from Jackson, MS, Jack Gray, and I were talking and he confirmed that Jackson was looking to hire another person in Branch Office Administration. He wanted to know if I would request a transfer to Jackson. He knew I might like to come to Jackson since I was originally from MS. I was definitely interested, because Kathy and I were both home sick. We would travel to visit our folks on a weekend just to spend a few hours with each of them. I applied for the transfer, and in two months we were looking for an apartment to rent near the IBM office in Jackson.

It was good to get out of the Signal Unit and back into my favorite Artillery Battalion (BN) headquartered in Newton, MS. I was assigned the BN S1, Personnel Officer. This was a much easier assignment than Ammunition Officer. I had a lot of exposure to Colonel Walker, our BN Commander. I also got to work again with Denver Brackeen, who had moved to the BN Staff and was promoted to Major. I also worked closely with the full-time staff.

I believe that being on the BN staff with exposure to the leaders of the BN is what led to a job offer to work full time for the National Guard at Newton, MS. Colonel Walker called me at work one day and asked me to have lunch with him. He lived in Jackson near the IBM office. I could not imagine why he was meeting with me. He offered me a full-time staff job with the rank of Major assigned to the BN staff in Newton, MS., Kathy's home town. I told Colonel Walker I would talk it over with Kathy. This would be a big raise for me compared to my salary at IBM, plus all the retirement benefits that go with a government job. Of course, giving up my IBM career, which I had dreamed of, was not an easy decision. Kathy was okay with me taking the job, but she said she really had no desire to live in Newton, MS. I was surprised, yet I had not had a big interest in living in Louisville either, having once turned down an interview to work with the Post Office. I talked with my brother, who had worked for the MS National Guard before being hired by IBM. He advised me not to take the job. It was political in many ways. You are actually working for the State of MS, not the US Government. I didn't take the position. I know I disappointed Colonel Walker.

I often wondered what it would have been like for me working for Colonel Walker. He became a General and was appointed Chief, National Guard Bureau, in Washington, the highest position there is for a National Guard Officer. He was actually a member of the Joint Chiefs of Staff for the Army. Denver Brackeen became a General and was appointed Adjutant General for the State of MS. I am sure had I done a good job I too would have made General. Having declined this big opportunity in the National Guard, I devoted my career priority to IBM.

I am glad that during the years of 1965 through 1967 I was in the Artillery BN. I enjoyed the "esprit de corps" with the unit. We were ordered to double our training to two weekends each month for a year in order to prepare for a possible call up for Vietnam. It was no fun thinking we may have to go to Vietnam, but if I had to go, it would be good to be with this unit. We never got activated, but we were ready. During this year of double training, Colonel Walker arranged for a Regular Army Artillery Test Team to conduct a test of our Artillery Group during our two week training at Camp Shelby, MS. During the test I was called on to perform an Air Forward Observer problem. We had never trained for this, but this was a critical role for the Forward Observer in Vietnam. I applied the rules I had learned at OCS. The difficulty was keeping the target in sight from a helicopter that was constantly moving. I did a perfect "Fire For Effect" and was sort of a hero for the Regular Army Test. Our unit passed the test with flying colors. That is proof of how dedicated the men of our unit were. They could have goofed off and failed the test on purpose, thinking it would save them from Vietnam.

At the end of 1967, IBM promoted me to Administration Operations Manager (AOM) Baton Rouge, LA. In four and a half years I had been made a manager in IBM. This resulted in moving from the MS National Guard to the Army Reserves because there were no Artillery units in the Baton Rouge area. I signed on to a Finance Unit, just right for my administrative skills. We did payroll. It was a small unit with 30 enlisted personnel and two officers. The Commanding Officer(CO) transferred out soon after I joined the unit, and I became the CO. This is the only command that I held during my entire military career. I attended the Army Finance

School at Fort Benjamin Harrison, IN, for training to become qualified as a Finance Officer. I had mixed emotions about having to exchange my Cannons for the Finance emblem. But finance was so much easier than artillery. We rode an air-conditioned bus to summer camp instead of a military vehicle convoy. My future as a finance officer turned out to be the best I could have ever hoped for. It was both easy and allowed me to experience some very interesting places that I would never have had the opportunity to train. Being in the Reserves rather than the National Guard allowed me to attend only the two weeks summer training each year rather than drill on a weekend of every month. This still provided enough points every year to have a good retirement year. My retirement income would not be as much. However, with my IBM retirement benefits I did not need to rely on the military. I no longer missed church and Bible study once a month.

For many years in the Reserves I was assigned to the Finance Office at Rock Island Arsenal in Rock Island, IL. This was an old, old military installation that was first opened during the Civil War and provided munitions for the US Army, not the Rebels. Its history included a prison for captured rebel soldiers. The arsenal is near the Mississippi River, which provided a means of transport for the munitions.

One year, another interesting assignment for me was to report to the Finance Office at Fort Mead, MD. This was a strategic Army base that produced highly classified research data for use by the military as well as the national security agencies. I was not exposed to anything classified. In fact, I was sent on a two week trip to audit the cash funds for units assigned to the Fort Mead Finance Office. These units were in the state of New York and had not been audited for several years. I had to account for the cash they had on hand and verify their expenditures were authorized. I inspected one unit in a very unsafe section of New York City. I had to call ahead in order for the full-time technician at the unit to raise the steel door for me to enter and close it behind me. I also audited a unit on the eastern tip of Long Island. I never knew that Long Island was so many miles long and so very narrow in places. I even traveled all the way to upstate New York to Fort Drum, famous for its heavy snows in winter. Soldiers always wanted to avoid Fort Drum because it was so isolated. I was exhausted from all the travel I had during that two week assignment.

Had I remained in Artillery I would have probably gone to the Army War College and been promoted to full Colonel. There were so few slots for full Colonel in Finance that I never applied for the War College. I retired after four years as an enlisted soldier and twenty eight as a commissioned officer. We enjoy a nice retirement check each month, and more importantly medical supplemental insurance that covers the balance that Medicare does not pay. This alone is worth the years I devoted to my military assignments and career.

I devoted a long Chapter to my military career because it has been very important in my life. I am very thankful that my brother recommended, and my parents signed, that I could join the National Guard at age seventeen and a half. We have been blessed in many ways by my military career. The pay enabled my first year at ECJC. Later, as an officer, the additional income allowed Kathy to be home with the children until they started school. Even then, she only worked part time jobs so she could be home when they got home from school, and also so that she could be off each summer. My years in the various assignments are special memories because of the many individuals that I had the privilege of knowing and working with. Many of them had a great impact on my life and I owe them a debt of gratitude for the trust and confidence they had in me. Men like Captain Blaylock who recommended me for OCS, General Denver Brackeen, my first CO, General Walker, the best leader I have ever known, Coach Billie Ray Lindsey, Warrant Officer and Newton High School football coach and Mr. Vance, also a Warrant Officer and full-time staff employee. These are just a few that stand out. They guided me from my youth to manhood and gave me opportunity after opportunity. They believed in me. We had many good times at the small Officers' Club at Camp Shelby, MS. We sang along when we played "Elvira" over and over on the jukebox and had a beer or two.

Chapter 15:

MEETING THE ONE

✥

When I arrived at Mom and Dad's from OCS, I had only three days before fall semester classes started at ECJC. This was just enough time to catch up on my sleep and tell Mom and Dad a little about how tough it was at OCS. I hardly had time to adjust into civilian life. I was still moving and conversing as if I was still

in the military. It took several days to become a civilian again.

Arriving on campus, I was pleasantly surprised to learn that I was assigned to the just completed new men's dorm, Todd Hall. It was nothing like the barracks dorm my Freshman year. It had suites of four adjoining private rooms with a huge shower for each suite. My roommate was an agreeable little guy about five feet tall, Roy Roberts. He was very friendly and a faithful Christian. Most of our suite mates were from Fairhope, AL.

I checked in with Mrs. Cross at the Student Center to get the details on my duties as postman. I would pick up the mail from the Decatur Post Office each morning, then deliver and distribute the mail to the office and to the students' mailboxes. This took only about an hour each day. I stayed for another hour and kept the Post Office open so that students could pick up packages mailed to them.

My Dad was very impressed that I was the Postman for the college. It was a very responsible job. While I was working in Forest, he told me about a postal civil service exam that was being given in Kosciusko, MS. I took off work and took the exam. I must have scored well, because when there was an opening at the Louisville Post Office, Dad called me and said the Postmaster, Boyd McMillan, asked if I would like to interview for the job. I turned him down. I know Mom and Dad were both very disappointed. I knew that a veteran would be given priority. That would have been my opportunity to have a career in my hometown, but I declined. I was determined to get my degree, but I was not sure what I might be successful in doing. Again, God had a different plan for my life.

I was an Accounting major with a minor in Finance. I enjoyed all my courses and made good grades. One course that I took which was not required, but was very beneficial, was Speech. I was always nervous when speaking to a group. It helped, but I never did become a relaxed public speaker. It was a fun class because each of us had to give a speech about something funny that had happened to us.

As in my first year, I did not date anyone. I did join the Baptist Student Union (BSU) and attended with Roy. We both had good friends in BSU. For the first time in a long time I did my Bible reading and prayer time as I had when I was growing up.

My second year flew by. I had the Post Office job every day, National Guard training every Monday night, my studies, football and basketball games, BSU and no lonely weekends at an empty college. Because most students went home every weekend, my first year I had to bum a ride or hitch hike. The weekends I had duty in the Student Center at the soda fountain I could not go home. The second year, since I had a car and my job ended by 10 am on Saturday, I had time to go home for some of Mother's great home cooked meals. Also, friends would ride with me, and I would drop them off and pick them up at their house on the return to ECJC.

I learned that I was not the only student from a financially poor family background. When I went home, I attended church with Mom and Dad at Evergreen. It was good to see all my friends in our church family.

Very soon after school started, I called up Sue Ellen to let her know how I was and to ask her if she would like to attend a football game at ECJC with me. After some persuading, she agreed. I wanted to show her off to my suite mates and possibly rekindle our romance. But the romance was not rekindled. She had a steady boyfriend that had a good job with the Singer Sewing Machine Company. Sue Ellen was still working at the jewelry store and was not interested in a boyfriend away at college. I was disappointed, but again God had another plan for my life. I kept her beautiful 8 by 10 picture displayed in my room for a long time.

Just prior to Christmas, I received a letter from Nancy. This was a real shock. I had not had any communication with her in almost three years. She was inviting me to attend the Sugar Bowl game in New Orleans on New Year's Day. That trip was presented in an earlier Chapter.

My busy routine continued the second semester with one addition. I joined Mr. Fick's choir at the insistence of my roommate, Roy. One evening after choir practice, I struck up a conversation with Kathy Rainer. Kathy and I talked as if we had known each other for years. We walked to the library together and stayed until it closed. I then walked her to her dorm. We had date night once a week at ECJC and you had to be back in the dorm by 10 pm. After two date nights, Kathy and I knew that we were falling in love. I soon was visiting in her home at Newton and meeting her Mom and Dad. Then she went to Louisville one weekend with me and stayed with my cousins that lived next door, Dixie, Linda and Billy. We went to church at Evergreen. I know I was smiling from ear to ear when I introduced her to many of my church family. This was only the second time I had a girl meet my parents and church family and see where I grew up. Kathy was so confident yet congenial. Her warm, sincere personality won over all the family. Everyone liked her after being with her only a short time. Over the years, she was very good with my Mother and Dad, always helping out in the kitchen and taking an interest in them. They always admired Kathy and believed God had provided my life partner.

I was always at ease with Kathy. She eliminated all of my self-conscious, inferiority complex and gave me a confidence that I had never experienced before. Kathy was a city girl, but not at all like Nancy. Kathy lived across the RR track instead of on the street with the society of Newton. Her house was an old one with character, but the furnishings were very much like ours. Their lot was large enough for a big garden spot and a small catfish pond. The train passed within fifty yards of their front porch. Kathy's mother worked at a pants factory. Her Dad was a painter and wall-paper hanger. He liked to play dominoes in the pool hall and go fishing with his partner, Mr. Amos, an attorney in town. Kathy was a straight A student, Newton High School Homecoming Queen, and winner of the Doolittle Cup, a local award given to outstanding graduates of Newton High School. She was a contestant in the Miss Newton beauty contest and was voted Miss Congeniality. She had worked summers during her high school years.

Before we met, Kathy had applied and received a band scholarship to Delta State Teachers College in Cleveland, MS. Kathy planned to be a teacher. With the help of Mrs. Cross, I applied and received a work scholarship to Delta State. By the time of my graduation at ECJC, I understood why God had arranged for me to take four years to obtain a two-year Junior College degree. I am sure that no one was as happy as Kathy and I on graduation day. We were graduating with honors, were in love and would be attending senior college together.

Chapter 16:

SUMMER OF 61

※

Kathy had a good summer job lined up working at the Sam B Reid Insurance Agency where her sister Joyce worked. I had interviewed for a summer job with the MS State Highway Department in Newton but had not been contacted about working. A new science building was contracted to be constructed on campus. I was hired to work on it. With pick and shovel we dug the trenches for pouring the foundation. This was back-breaking manual labor. I lived in the dorm for free thanks to Denver Brackeen and Coach Blount. Thankfully, it was only a couple of weeks before I was hired by the MS Highway Department. I would work with a survey crew preparing right of way survey data for Interstate 20 crossing MS east to west. This was not easy work, sometimes cutting a path with a machete for the survey line of sight recordings. I qualified for this kind of work because of my experience in Artillery. We had to survey in the gun positions so that the Fire Direction Center had initial data to work with in computing the correct data to the guns from the Forward Observer. Once again, the military had been beneficial. Kathy and I exchanged letters every week, sometimes writing every night. We dated every weekend. She would ride the bus from Jackson to Newton, and I would take her back to Jackson on Sunday night. My gas guzzling 88 Olds was not letting me put away any savings for college. My priority was to be with Kathy when possible.

For her birthday on August 7th, I bought her a birthstone ring at the little jewelry store next door to the Five and Dime where I had worked during high school. Later that month, we were parked at the little drive-in hamburger joint in Newton, very much like the A-1 drive-in in Louisville. We were talking about Delta State in Cleveland, MS, and that it would soon be time for us to leave for school. Suddenly, without previously planning or even thinking, I blurted out, "Let's not go to college. Let's get married." Without any hesitation Kathy said "OK!" I think God Himself must have given me that most casual of all "casual" proposals ever. We were both working and making money, and both wanted to get married.

The very next weekend we were in Jackson at Wilson's Wholesale picking out a set of rings. This is where I, with no experience with weddings, should have consulted Kathy's family about setting dates. Instead I went about giving Kathy her engagement ring the following 7th, which was September. I had this thing about the 7th. I'm not sure if I asked Kathy when the wedding date should be. I think I just arbitrarily set the date for October 7th, a Saturday. I know this caused everyone undue stress to get a wedding together that quick, but dumb me had not given any thought to what was required to put on a church wedding. Kathy, nor any of her family, ever complained to me once about this rushed up ceremony. I am sure there were some that thought we had probably messed up and had to get married. But that was not the case. We just did not want to wait. Kathy's mother worked in a factory. Her only time off was when the plant closed down in the summer for two weeks. Kathy and Joyce put the entire wedding together from the Sam B Reid Insurance Agency. They got the permission of the boss to spend time working on the wedding plans. Kathy remained in that job until we moved to Little Rock, when I was hired by IBM. Sam B.

Reid gave her a glowing recommendation when she applied and was hired by Prudential in Little Rock. She always gave one hundred per cent plus to every job she performed.

Proud Parents and Kathy's Grandmother on our Wedding Day

Our wedding was small, very informal, and above all, inexpensive. Neither set of parents had extra money for a wedding. Kathy and I had none. There were no invitations, only an announcement in the Newton Record, the local weekly newspaper. Had we been able to afford a formal, planned well in advance wedding, I know we would have had a church full. Kathy's family had many friends and relatives, and I had a number of friends in Newton and Decatur because of my job in the National Guard with our Headquarters at Newton. There were also many friends from my church in Evergreen. We had the right wedding for us at the time, with only our immediate families. Joyce was Kathy's Maid of

Honor and Carey was my Best Man. Joyce's husband, Charles, a Baptist Preacher, performed the ceremony. Kathy's Aunt Jewel prepared a delicious meal for our reception at her home. She was the sweetest person you would ever meet. She was in a wheelchair but lived alone and did everything for herself. We would visit her when we came to Newton to visit Kathy's parents.

Happy Newly Weds on October 7, 1961

In 2011, we celebrated our 50th Wedding Anniversary in style and made up big time for our skimpy wedding.

Chapter 17:

HONEYMOONING IN FLORIDA – NOT REALLY

Not only was I not any help planning our wedding, my plan for a honeymoon did not exist. When we up and decided to get married instead of attending Delta State, it was imperative that I land a good job in Jackson. Kathy had already been hired by Sam B. Reid Insurance when she told them she was getting married and needed a job. Kathy's sister, Joyce, like my brother, Carey, had been helpful in so many ways, like the great summer job and now full-time employment. With my Junior College degree in Accounting, I thought an accounting firm would be anxious to hire me. I interviewed with the only one that was advertising. They preferred Senior College graduates. I saw an ad by Lester Engineering for Survey crews. I interviewed and was hired since I had experience working with the MS Highway Department on a survey crew. I would again be swinging a machete. But at least we both had jobs, both making $50 a week, when I got in a full 40 hours work. The problem with my job was that we didn't work when it rained. The one month I worked before we got married was not enough time to save money for a honeymoon. Most of my paycheck went to pay for room and board at a boarding house. I had very little cash. This was before I had a credit card, even one for gasoline. Our honeymoon would be like our wedding, very inexpensive. But we didn't mind, we were in love. We would have been happy if we had eloped and used an Alabama Justice of the Peace to perform the ceremony. This is what Kathy's brother, Jerry, and his wife, Bitsy, had done.

After the wonderful meal prepared by Aunt Jewel, we said goodbye to Mom and Dad, Carey and the few relatives that had come from Louisville to the wedding. We then went over to Kathy's house and loaded her lone suitcase. As we were hugging our good-bye's, Mr. Rainer slipped me a twenty dollarbill. I am sure he didn't know just how badly I needed that twenty bucks.

We drove south on MS Highway 15 through Laurel and stopped in Hattiesburg for a burger at Shoney's. Don't ask me why I was hungry after the fine meal at Aunt Jewel's. I think I was so nervous and busy talking with everyone after the wedding that I failed to eat very much. It was late afternoon when we arrived in Gulfport and dark before we found a hotel with a vacancy. After checking in, I think we ate at a restaurant. I cannot recall if we did or not and if we did, I don't know the kind of restaurant nor what we ate.

It was probably 9 pm when we were in the room and ready to get into bed. I didn't bring PJ's, so I was undressed and in bed in a minute. Kathy went into the bathroom to dress for bed. It seemed like she stayed a long time. When she finally came out, she was dressed in this beautiful pink gown with matching house robe over the gown. She was beautiful and I knew she had bought this new beautiful outfit for this special night. But, she was crying.

I didn't know if this was normal for a girl on her wedding night or what. I could not think of anything to say except, "What is wrong Kathy?" She blurted out that her period had started. I am certain I am the only newlywed that spent his first honeymoon night out looking for a store that was open that sold Tampax. I assured her it would be fine if we had to wait another week. I may have been somewhat relieved since I was already a nervous wreck. She said the excitement of the wedding caused her period to start early. I think It was because I had picked the wedding day of October 7 without consulting anyone and certainly not considering any such item as when Kathy would have her period. I had not given any time for anyone to do much planning. I think God used this to teach me the proper response when Kathy was upset and crying. Our sleep that night was not very restful. However, we knew we didn't have to worry about her getting pregnant on our wedding night. Carey had loaded my suitcase with rubbers (a.k.a. condoms) but they could wait for another day.

The next morning, I don't recall breakfast. I had the bright idea to drive to the panhandle of Florida. Then we could say we went to Florida on our honeymoon. We drove to Pensacola and walked on the beach. It was cold and windy. We then headed home. That night we looked and looked for a motel with a vacancy, and finally ended up at a dump. We should have planned to drive all the way to Louisville on Sunday night and stay at Mom and Dad's instead of staying on the road that night. We only had the one day off, Monday. We got to Louisville at noon on Monday and enjoyed one of Mother's wonderful meals. As we were leaving, Dad slipped me a twenty dollar bill. It was a life saver. I had to use five of it for gas to get to Jackson.

We stopped at Winston Furniture Company and bought a Muntz black and white TV. The TV was the only item we owned in our furnished three-room apartment. Zero down and pay each month any amount we could afford. How is that for friends. The Muntz lasted a very long time. It still worked when we got our first color TV years later. We arrived at our Jackson apartment late Monday afternoon and began our life together at 133 1/3 South Prentiss Street.

Chapter 18:

133 1/3 PRENTISS STREET

❊

O ur unique address came about because the landlady had her home at 133. She converted a garage next to her house into a two-story apartment. Since it was not a different lot, the Post Office assigned the two apartments 133 1/3 and 133 2/3. Our rent was only forty five dollars per month plus utilities. It was three small rooms, kitchen, living room and bedroom and a tiny bathroom. We owned no furniture except for the Muntz TV. The kitchen had a metal table and four chairs. The living room had a couch and table for the TV. The bedroom had a regular bed, a dresser and a small closet. The bathroom only had a shower. We only ate supper in the little apartment. We usually went to either Kathy's folks or my folks on weekends, and we brought back their great cooking which lasted us a couple of days. Kathy ate cereal for breakfast. I would get a sweet roll and coke when the survey crew stopped at a convenience store to buy our lunch, which was usually Vienna sausage and crackers and another sweet roll. Kathy rode the bus to work. We were only a block off West Capital Street, so it was convenient for her to catch the bus.

I had National Guard on Monday nights, so I drove to Decatur and back. This was before the Guard started drilling one weekend each month. Kathy went with me a few times and visited with her folks. Later, I car pooled with two other guys living in Jackson that were in Service Battery. At this time I was still the Ammunition Officer. As an Officer, I was getting a good paycheck every quarter for my National Guard duty. My Lester Engineering hourly pay job lacked a dependable paycheck.

If it rained, we couldn't work. Around Jackson it rains a lot in the winter. When we were not working, I was applying for a better job. I landed a job at Storkline Corp., a manufacturing plant that made baby furniture, sewing machine cabinets and the product in strong demand, TV cabinets. They made TV cabinets for RCA, Sears, all the name brand TV's. I worked in Production Control. We kept manual running inventory of all the parts for the manufacturing lines. This was before they had data processing for inventory control. We manually counted daily and ordered parts to be manufactured based on the backlog of cabinets yet to be built for a particular style. This inventory also included work in process. It was a boring job but also very critical. If the line ran out of parts for a cabinet that was in production, the entire line went down, and several employees were idle. The plant was a dusty, dirty environment. All the parts were wood. My job was not real dusty, except when I had to inventory the work in process on the line. When the parts were manufactured, sawing and sanding required the workers to wear masks. Their masks and head would be covered in dust. Considering this manufacturing plant, I had one of the better jobs.

Not long after I started at Storkline, there was an unusual weather event for Jackson, MS. It came a snow blizzard. It started about noon one day, and by 3 pm the snow was three inches deep, which completely shut down the city of Jackson. They had not one snow plow or salt truck. Businesses started sending everyone home by 4 pm, but it was too late. The cars could not go in the snow. There were no front wheel or 4-wheel drive vehicles back then. A few that had chains were all that could move. The trip from the plant to the apartment was about five miles. I only got about three miles, then everything was blocked. We all abandoned our cars and started walking to our destinations. I arrived at the apartment after dark. Kathy was home. Someone in their office had a Jeep and had delivered several of the workers to their homes. The next morning, we had icicles three feet long hanging from our little apartment roof. The sun was shining and the snow was melting, so we walked to get our car. The blizzard of 1962 was in the record books.

The Blizzard of 1962

Kathy and I never discussed our money. We at this point paid cash for everything. I did get a Texaco credit card. I never wanted to be stranded because I ran out of gas, as I almost did on our honeymoon. From the very beginning, we pooled our money in one bank account and if anything cost very much, we talked about it to make sure we really needed it. Many times I was rude to Kathy because she would admire something in the store window and say, "Isn't that pretty or nice?" I would quip, "You don't need that!" Actually all she meant was that she liked it. I think I was disappointed that I could not afford it for her. We were both surprised that we had saved five hundred dollars in six months. So, in May 1962, we purchased our first house at 124 Whitehall Avenue in Southwest Jackson. Our down payment of five hundred dollars left a mortgage of twelve thousand dollars. Our house payment was sixty five dollars per month. We didn't have a stick of furniture, but we had a house and a Muntz TV.

Our First House

Chapter 19:

NEW FURNITURE, NEW JOB, NEW CAR, NIGHT SCHOOL

The bold step of home ownership set off a number of changes to our circumstances. Before moving into our new to us, used house, we had to furnish it. We needed every room of furniture for two bedrooms, living room and kitchen with eating area. My friend Pruitt Calvert at Winston Furniture Company in Louisville immediately came to mind. We had paid off the Muntz TV in record time so he could trust us with credit. On the weekend, we visited the furniture store and determined that Pruitt would deliver the furniture to Jackson for no charge and again we could pay any amount as we were able. We shopped all day trying to visualize how each item we needed would fit into our rooms. We purchased two beds with mattresses, two dressers, a dinette table with four chairs and a couch and two chairs for the living room. I don't know how, but Pruitt backed into our driveway with all of that furniture loaded on a pickup. It was a full load. We used that load of furniture for many years. Most of it moved from Jackson to Little Rock, back to Jackson, from Jackson to Baton Rouge and again back to Jackson. We didn't wear the furniture out. It was worn out from moving.

As soon as we were settled in our new home, we realized there were some problems related to where we had chosen to live. My work was now about ten miles across town. Kathy's bus ride to her downtown office went through the predominately black section of town, including the all black, Jackson State University. Our move coincided with the racial tensions throughout the South in the Spring of 1962. James Meredith was enrolling at Ole Miss, escorted by US Marshals. President Kennedy, in order to prevent Governor Ross Barnett from sending the MS National Guard to Ole Miss, federalized the MS National Guard and we sat at the National Guard Armory the week that Meredith was enrolled. The MS National Guard was also called out to assist the Jackson Police Department control the riots at Jackson State two weeks later. We did not anticipate that it would not be safe on the bus ride for Kathy into town until all of this happened. Initially, I tried driving her to town then back out to the Storkline plant. This trip took an hour in rush hour traffic and the same for the return trip.

We decided I should look for a job near Kathy's office. Then we could go to work together, and our commute time and distance would be a snap. I interviewed and landed a job at the Emporium, the elite department store in downtown. This was the most boring job one could imagine. I worked in the delivery department. The well-to-do of Jackson would call their order in or shop, then have the order delivered to their home. There were two delivery trucks, one for South and one for North. We would route the packages to the correct delivery truck as they came down on the dumbwaiter. Most of the time was spent checking the address to make certain we put the package on the correct truck. The delivery guys knew all their repeat customers, and they would spot a package immediately if it didn't belong to their route. This job helped my night school grades, because I could study during the idle time. I would complain about no work to do and Kathy would complain that she had too much work. It was great to ride to work together and have lunch together. This made a boring job worthwhile.

At this time, the Olds 88, now six years old, began to have problems- fuel pump, carburetor, problems that would cause the motor to quit and not start back up. This was dangerous, and repair work was expensive. We also needed new tires. We walked into the Chevrolet dealer down the street from where we worked and purchased a Chevy II off the show room floor. It was a tan, four door, 6 cylinder, very economical car compared to the 88. The smaller car served us well for many years. It was probably the best car decision I would ever make. It was our first new car, and we picked it out together. With the 88 trade in on an inexpensive car, our monthly payments were very manageable. I was still traveling to National Guard in Decatur every Monday night, so the car was ideal for that 120 mile round trip.

The night I enrolled in night school at Mississippi College, a Baptist College in Clinton, MS, ten miles west of Jackson, I ran into Raymond. He was from Louisville, and we had met at ECJC. I learned he worked as an accountant in Jackson. He had married Evelyn. Her family lived on Brooksville Road, south of our farm. Small world. We became friends with them, and Raymond and I would sometimes study together. We both had to take Old and New Testament, required studies at the Baptist College. Having attended church all my young life and studied the Bible, the courses were easy for me. I was a great help to him.

Once during this first year of our marriage, I created a real crisis. In 1962 the MS National Guard was activated for an emergency in Natchez, MS. We were responsible for evacuation of part of the city near the MS River where a chlorine barge had sunk. If the gas should escape into the water, it would become a poison gas. While in Natchez, a buddy and I rode downtown and parked at a burger drive-in. A car pulled up beside us and we started talking to two nice young ladies. Back then, the drive-in was the place to go to meet potential dates. After some conversation, we ended up in the car with them and learned they were both schoolteachers. They were impressed that we were officers with the National Guard on duty for the potential chlorine disaster. We ended up making a date with them for the very next night. We got their phone number and address and set a time we would pick them up. When we got back to camp, I realized I did not want to go through with this very wrong plan. My Christian upbringing won out over the devil's temptation. God had not deserted me even though I had drifted away from Him.

God had an unbelievable plan to fix my sinful situation. We had a new officer in the unit who was single. I explained my situation and with a little pleading, I convinced him to go on this blind date in my place. And he did. This was truly God taking over to save me from sin and possibly to save my marriage. When I got home, I explained to Kathy exactly what had happened, for I knew she and her family in Newton would find out from the National Guard guys what I had done. I told her I was very sorry and that it would never happen again. She cried and thanked me for telling her. I know she was disappointed in my even thinking of doing such a thing. I made it up to her by always being faithful to her. I learned an important lesson and realized how easy it is to be led astray. We had a big GOD THING moment when we learned that the lady and young officer that replaced me on the date were getting married.

I have practically no memory of how Kathy was coping with all the time when I was away for National Guard duty during this year. After all, we had only been married less than a year. She was continuing to work and never complained. She understood my commitment to the National Guard, and I always emphasized the fact that the income I earned was very beneficial and allowed us to afford night school. With this pace in our lives at this time we did not take the time to find and become active in a church. When we did have a free weekend, we would visit her folks or my folks and attend church with them. Not aware of it then, but looking back, I feel we were moving away from God and our upbringing in the church. I know I was not putting God first in my life. But God never was far from us. He continued to guide our lives, and many times He brought us back to Him at times when I thought I was in complete control.

Shortly after we married, I interviewed with IBM at the Jackson Branch Office. Since my brother was hired by IBM in early 1960, it was my goal to someday work for IBM. It was one of the fastest growing companies in the world. I was not hired. Their letter stated they would contact me if there was an opening. Finally, in early 1962, I received a call to come in for an interview. The interview went well, but at the end they asked if I would be willing to move to New Orleans. I am sure that the disappointment showing on my face and that I answered that I preferred to work in Jackson is the reason I was not hired for New Orleans. Later, my boss in Jackson who had been an Administrative Operations Manager (AOM) in New Orleans, told me I was not hired because they knew I did not want to live in New Orleans.

A few months later, in May 1963, my brother called and said there was an administrative position open in Little Rock, Arkansas. I interviewed and of course I was hired, because they knew I would be an excellent employee because of the example set by my brother, Carey. I was one of very few hired by IBM without a college degree. This began a tremendous thirty-year career with a very, very great company. This was even greater than graduating from OCS and receiving my commission. At age 24, this country bumpkin from the red clay hills of Mississippi was now working for the most prestigious company in the United States.

Chapter 20:

HIRED BY IBM – WOW

⊁⊀

After only one year in our first house, it went up for sale. We were moving to Little Rock, AK. In 1963 the easy way to sell a house was to have someone assume your loan. That is what we did. No waiting for loan approvals. We asked for five hundred down and received it, which was the amount we had paid down. We rented a U-Haul Truck and loaded it with the furniture we bought at Winston Furniture Company. Carey and Betty came and helped us load. We left Jackson about 6 pm on a Saturday afternoon and drove into the next morning. Betty drove their car, Kathy our Chevy II, Carey and I shared driving the truck. We were all exhausted from loading our furniture and driving half the night.

We rented an apartment in Little Rock on the first floor of a two-story building with eight apartments on each floor. We unloaded Sunday afternoon and were at work Monday morning. Within a week, Kathy had interviewed at Prudential Insurance and was hired based on the very favorable recommendation from Sam B. Reid Insurance Company. In a short time, she was secretary to the manager for Prudential in Little Rock. The Prudential office was near the IBM office, so we rode to work together.

It is ironic that my brother, Carey, Kathy's brother, Jerry, and I all got our career starts in Little Rock and lived there at the same time. My brother was first hired by IBM, then Jerry was hired by the US Corp of Engineers and then I was hired by IBM. Having family nearby was truly a blessing for us. Carey and Betty had a little boy, Randy, 18 months old and Jerry and Bitsy had their first child, Allyson.

Kathy and I went home to visit our folks as often as we could. One Christmas, we drove late into the night on snow covered highways that had not been touched by a snowplow. All we had were two ruts to drive in, and if we met another vehicle, we had to share one of the ruts with them. It took twice as long, but we made it without an accident. Later we thought about how foolish we were. God was watching over us, I know.

My IBM Career started in the back of the IBM office in the Parts and Supplies room. It was adjacent to the shop, which was a work space for customer engineers to bring in typewriters or data processing machines that they were unable to repair in the customer's office. I worked the process desk for all orders and supply agreements for office products, mainly typewriter ribbons and type elements, the famous round ball of letters on the Selectric typewriter. I took the order by phone or letters, packed, weighed, stamped, typed the invoice that produced the packing slip, and shipped all the supplies for the State of Arkansas. I was as busy as a one-armed paper hanger. Then once a month I shipped supply agreements. These were annual agreements with periodic supply shipments that were sold by the marketing representatives. The supply agreement gave the customer a quantity discount based on the annual total.

A couple of weekends we looked for a house and found a new development near my brother's neighborhood and signed a contract to build a house on Oakwood Street. We didn't have any savings, but with both of us working for elite companies, we had no problem qualifying for a loan for a fifteen thousand dollar new home. Within six months after moving to Little Rock, we moved into our first, but not the last, spanking new home. The house had a nice living room where I did most of my study and accounting homework for night school at Little Rock University (LRU).

I had enrolled for the fall semester majoring in Finance and Accounting. LRU accepted all my credits from MS College except the six hours of Bible that was required at MS College. One semester I took three courses, thinking Economics would be a snap. We studied two theories, and on the exam I wrote answers confusing the two theories, so my answers were all wrong. The only course I ever flunked in all my years of school. It was a major embarrassment for me. IBM paid 75% of my tuition if I made C or better. I had to submit my grades in order to be paid for the two that I passed. Accounting was my favorite, but it required a lot of homework. I know Kathy got bored on weekends with my National Guard duties one weekend every month plus the weekend home-work. I think Kathy got interested in accounting while helping me, for she had always planned to be a teacher. When she returned to college, she majored in Accounting rather than teaching. She loved accounting work, and she became a very successful CPA. This was another example of God in control of our lives taking us beyond any dream we could have ever imagined.

God was pouring out blessing after blessing upon us, but I was not aware of giving Him very much credit. I felt in complete control, and I was making all the right decisions. After almost two years of marriage, we had yet to be a part of any church family. Only occasionally had we visited a church and were never having a daily devotion time. We prayed often for our aging parents and for our safety and health, rather selfish petitions. After getting set-tled in our new home, even with our hectic schedule, we committed to getting connected to a good church and attend regularly. We found a medium size church that we liked, especially the young preacher's sermons. The devil stepped right into our lives in a direct way. The pastor ran off with the music director, and I was really upset. I used it as an excuse to decide I did not need church. We never went back to that church. It would be eight years before we became active and finally became part of a church family.

Our first two years of marriage were filled with turmoil. Our marriage was fine, but the outside world was depressing to say the least. In 1962, MS was in the national news almost daily for civil rights clashes, riots and deaths. We had both grown up isolated from the plight of the Black race living in our communities. We had no idea of their feelings of discrimination they experienced. We were taught that all things were separate but equal. It was all taken for granted this was the way it was. A black family lived one fourth mile from our house where I grew up, but we had no association with them. Once Dad believed the black man stole one of our cows. Dad found the cow at the person's farm that bought the cow, but the man never admitted that he knew the cow was stolen when he bought it. Dad got his cow back but did not approach the black man about the theft. With the Ole Miss enrollment of James Meredith, I was directly involved when President Kennedy federalized the National Guard to prevent the MS Governor from calling us up to block the enrollment. Kathy and I both had some serious discussions with friends and relatives about the terrible situation in MS. In Arkansas we were embarrassed to let anyone know we were from MS. Then, with the assassination of Dr. Martin Luther King Jr. in Memphis and all the riots of devastation in the major cities, it was as if the country was falling apart. Then came the riots in Chicago at the Democratic Convention. College campuses became a hotbed of protesters for any and everything. The "anything goes" generation was born, and all the sexual boundaries covered in the Bible and taught by the church cast aside as no longer relevant. Our world and what we had been taught was being turned upside down.

At the IBM office, the customer engineers played a radio when they were working on machines in the shop. When President Kennedy was shot, the entire office gathered around that little white radio and heard the horrible news. The following long Thanksgiving holiday weekend we sat horrified watching TV as Jack Ruby shot Lee Harvey Oswald. It was played over and over. It was a Thanksgiving that was anything but Thanksgiving.

With all this going on and with the Presidential election on the horizon, I happened to see Ronald Reagan's speech for Barry Goldwater. I believed this had to be the answer to all the turmoil in our country. I became a lifelong Republican. I campaigned for Goldwater by distributing twenty-five copies of a paperback entitled "A Texan Looks at Lyndon." This was the true story of Lyndon Johnson demanding that the pilot of a small plane come to pick him up at his ranch during stormy weather. The plane went down, and the pilot lost his life. The book didn't help much. I think Goldwater only won two states, one being the state of Mississippi.

Early in 1965, I flew to New Orleans to attend an IBM training class for implementing automation procedures for the Supply Agreement operation. The plane was a Delta, DC8, twin engine prop. On the return trip we flew into a thunder storm, and the pilot had to land at Fort Polk, LA to wait out the storm. Needless to say, I was a bit nervous. I had many more harrowing, white knuckle flights in my future travels during my IBM career. I did some of my most sincere praying on some of those flights. I know my Mom and Dad prayed for my safety, for I always told them when I was scheduled to fly. At the meeting, I met and became friends with Jack Gray from Jackson, MS. I told him about interviewing in Jackson and how much I would like to work there. He suggested I put in a request for transfer, which I had not heard about. When there was an opening, priority would be given to me. All we needed to do was explain we needed to be near our aging parents. So, I put in the request, and within a few months I was offered a job in the

IBM office in Jackson. They were no longer in the office down-town. IBM had built an award winning designed new office in north Jackson. By October 1965, we moved to Jackson and I began working in the IBM Office. This had been my dream for a long time.

Kathy was very successful at Prudential. She was promoted to Secretary to the President, Mr. Penson. They were disappointed that she was leaving but understood why we needed to move. Prudential immediately transferred her to Jackson. She continued to work for Prudential until we moved to Baton Rouge, a wonderful career of over five years. She made many friends at Prudential.

We had mixed emotions on leaving Little Rock. It was won-derful being close to our family members, Carey and Betty, Jerry and Bitsy, our nephew Randy and niece Alyson. Kathy and I had talked it over and knew this was what we both wanted to do. It turned out to be a terrific move for my IBM career. The adminis-tration manager in Little Rock, Don Clough, was very old school and strait-laced. He did not communicate much with the employees. My new administration manager in Jackson took an early interest in me and became my mentor to become a manager. He was very outgoing and communicated daily with all the administrators. It was fun working for him.

I was also excited to be returning to the MS National Guard Artillery unit. Artillery was my first love in the National Guard, and I had many friends in the unit. There was a lot of camaraderie. I had transferred to a Signal unit in the Arkansas National Guard when we moved to Little Rock. I was not qualified for the Signal Branch. I was glad to be back with the big guns. Little did I know that we would be training two weekends every month for an entire year in preparation for us to go to Vietnam. The move to Jackson was also a boost for my military career.

Our time in Arkansas was not our favorite two years. The ter-rible events on the national scene, the turmoil, demonstrations, rioting and assassinations were depressing. They were constant reminders that all was not well with our country, as we had assumed throughout the 50's. We were very blessed to be with outstanding corporations and shielded from any hardships that were being suffered by many in our country during this time. We should have been in church every Sunday. However, we were too busy putting ourselves first. We did hold on to our basic Christian beliefs that our parents and church training had taught us.

We did visit some beautiful mountain scenery in the Ozarks. We had never been in the mountains. We actually saw the Arkansas hillbilly standing by the road with his gun. It was fun having our folks come to Arkansas for visits and taking them to see the mountain scenery. Kathy and I spent most of our free time together enjoying each others company. Kathy learned to bake Mom's pecan pie and cook chicken and dumplings as she practiced in her beautiful new kitchen on weekends.

It was a dream come true to be back in our home state of Mississippi.

Chapter 21:

AN IBM MANAGER – WOW

⊨⊨

We rented an older, large two-story home in the Belhaven neighborhood of north Jackson near the IBM office. I have two very unpleasant memories of this house. There were large trees around the house with leaves on the ground in the backyard. Roaches lived in the leaves. You could hear them moving around under the leaves. Another sad memory is that Mrs. Rainer slipped on the wooden stairs when visiting us and broke her ankle. It was a really bad break and did not heal correctly. It gave her pain the rest of her life.

We searched for a house to buy soon after moving. We found a small community of homes on Clubview Drive, off Old Canton Road. It faced the Jackson Country Club Golf Course. There was a tall fence to keep the stray golf balls from landing in the community. Only one lot remained, a corner lot. Our builder was the best person we could have ever expected to build a house. He wanted to build it exactly the way we wanted it. He would call and make suggestions and ask if we would like to have this or that. It was a pleasure doing business with him. The house was very nice.

Mr. Rainer gave us a pecan tree sprout that grew up from his pecan tree. When we were by the house many years later, the tree had grown to a be a huge, lovely tree. I feel that tree was for his memory, for we lost him to cancer at the young age of 66.

The Jackson office was much more relaxed compared to Little Rock, friendly and more fun at work. I was assigned to the Office Products Maintenance Agreement Desk. I maintained the agreements for inspection and repair of all the typewriters installed in the state of MS. These contracts were sold by the Customer Engineers (CE's) and Sales Reps. The contract gave the customer periodic inspections and maintenance of their typewriters, plus free service calls if the machine needed repair. This contract file was automated. I had to keep it current with new contracts or removals if a contract was canceled or amended. This automated file produced the monthly billing, so it required complete accuracy at all times, otherwise the customer's invoice would be wrong. Years later, this file would become a key factor for a major milestone in my IBM career.

Shortly after I returned to Jackson, a new Administration Manager, Ernest Mercer, was promoted to Jackson from New Orleans. He was young, very personable, and unlike the Admin Manager in Little Rock, he communicated with the Admin Staff daily. Soon after he came, the person that did Data Processing (DP) Orders and Movements transferred to the Montgomery, AL office. Ernest asked me to move to the DP orders and movements desk. This was the most responsible administration desk in the office. I processed the detailed and complex orders for computers. An order for a DP Installation would consist of several large machines, usually a processor, sorter, key punch and a collator. These orders were shipped on a moving van. I not only ordered but kept track of the schedule and coordinated the installation with the salesman and moving van company. All products were leased at this time, so the installation had to be installed by a specific date in order to prevent lost revenue. The IBM 360 was announced when I was on the desk. It was the most advanced DP Processing System available. Sales soared. A second person was added to the DP Orders and Movements Desk. We worked overtime to keep up with the order volumes. The desk had measurements for order accuracy and for timely installations. There was a contest between offices in our Region and we won two times. One prize I received was a small 12-inch TV. We used that little TV on the kitchen counter for many years. I also won a tailored suit. We all had to wear white shirts, tie and a suit to work. This was the best suit I have ever owned. I wore it for many years. Even after it was worn out, I kept it as a keepsake to remind me of the success I had in Jackson on the DP Order and Movements Desk.

Ernest and his wife Kate became friends with Kathy and me. On occasions, they invited us to their home prior to eating out with them. They would have a drink before we left, so we joined them. Since we didn't usually drink, we always had them make it more orange juice or 7-up than liquor. Ernest invited us to go to New Orleans for a weekend with them. Having lived in New Orleans, they wanted to take us to some of their favorite restaurants. He had just bought a new Buick Le Sabre. On the way to NO he swerved to miss a dog and slid on the wet pavement into a deep ditch. The highway was wet from a drizzling rain. The car was not damaged, but we were stuck. A farmer came and pulled us out with his tractor. We went on to NO and enjoyed some great food at the famous restaurants.

Before moving from Little Rock, I had completed almost enough hours at Little Rock University (LRU) to graduate. In the fall, after moving to Jackson, I enrolled again at MS College to take the required courses I needed to graduate from LRU with a degree in Finance and minor in Accounting. This would be an ideal degree for a management position in IBM. After transferring my additional credits from MS College to LRU in May 1967, we traveled to Little Rock in order for me to march down and receive my hard-earned degree. My six years of night school had all been worth it. It was a momentous day for me. Carey and Betty and

Mom and Dad attended the graduation ceremony. Finally, Kathy and I would not be working on homework during our weekends. Neither of us at this point dreamed that Kathy would be receiving her degree in Accounting, "summa cum laude," nine years later.

Graduation from Little Rock University, May, 1967

After earning my degree, I was more confident dealing with my associates in IBM. Almost all of the employees had college degrees. Everyone was happy for me and probably knew better than I did that Ernest was mentoring me for management. I was completely taken by surprise when Ernest called me into his office in November and asked if I would like to interview for the Administration Operations Manager (AOM) position in Baton Rouge, LA. What was running through my mind was if I would be qualified and ready to manage people. IBM was growing rapidly, and with the success of the IBM 360 System, the volumes were creating a need for Administration to add headcount, which led to the need for more managers. I was at the right place at the right time. Of course I would gladly interview for the AOM job. The interview with Frank Duke, the Administration Manager, was successful. God was again working in our lives but letting me believe I was in control.

We were sad leaving Jackson. We had made many friends. We saw our folks often. We loved our house and where we lived. I would miss the Artillery unit in Newton. I faced going from the known to the unknown, but I knew that if I was going to advance my career in IBM, I needed to take advantage of the opportunities when presented. Kathy had already planned to resign from Prudential before the arrival of our first child. With my promotion to management, she could be a stay at home Mom. We could still visit our folks often, for we were only a five-hour drive away. With the excitement and challenge of a new baby, a new job, and a new place to live, I launched my IBM Management career.

Chapter 22:

BATON ROUGE – A SPORTSMAN'S PARADISE

I was working in Baton Rouge by December 1, 1967. Kathy was six months pregnant. Our first priority was to find a house and get moved and settled before time for the baby, due in March. I picked out a few for Kathy to come and see. IBM flew her on her first airplane flight to look for a house. We settled on a roomy brick house in a young neighborhood on Nancy Drive. I didn't mention it to Kathy, but the street was the same name as my high school girl-friend! We could now get moved and have the baby nursery set up just in time. We didn't know if it was a boy or girl. This was before all the scans were available. Even though Kathy was still working at Prudential and was very pregnant, she took care of everything that had to get done for the move. I know she worked many hours, but, again, not a single complaint or phone call in distress. She was always supportive and took care of all the details in every one of our three more moves with IBM. We were settled in our house by mid-February. IBM took care of selling the house in Jackson.

We had visits from both Kathy's parents and my parents in early March to check out our new place. We had to show them the one sight of interest in Baton Rouge, which was the State Capitol

Building. The bullet holes where Huey Long was shot are still in the wall. Long was the colorful Louisiana Senator that controlled the political agenda for Louisiana. Kathy walked too much on Sunday showing them the sights.

On Monday morning, March 11, 1968, she had labor pains, and we were at Woman's Hospital by eight am. But not until eight pm did our precious little boy, Ronald Lee Livingston, arrive. I was a nervous wreck after waiting all day, not knowing what was happening and not able to be with Kathy. This was before fathers were allowed to be part of the birthing scene. Kathy had a hard time, and we stayed an extra day in the hospital to get her recovered. We got little sleep the first few nights. Lee had colic for several weeks, and it took several tries to find a formula that his little premature stomach could handle. He had arrived about three weeks early and needed more time to be ready for good digestion.

Kathy had made friends with a neighbor, Gail Beaupre. She had two small children and she was a big help for Kathy. My boss's wife, Jenola, was also a big help. She had three small children, so she knew the answer for every problem situation that came up. We were very thankful for their phone and hands-on support. We remained close friends with the two families for many years.

Meanwhile, I came down with a rare disease. My beard stopped growing in spots on my face. Small round white spots appeared. I made an appointment with a doctor to get it checked. He asked if any traumatic events had happened to me. I explained I had just moved, had a new job, and my wife had just had a baby. He said, " Your face will clear up in a few weeks." And it did.

The Baton Rouge office environment was different in many ways from either Jackson or Little Rock. The major accounts were oil refineries. Their computers had to be up and running 24/7. If the refinery had to be shut down it was bad, bad news. There was a tremendous pressure on everyone. The orders and movements function was handled by three capable individuals. Two did only the refineries and one handled all the other accounts. Ken Reid was the expert for the refineries. All of his orders for the refineries were, Request for Price Quote (RPQ's), for they had to be custom built. The salesmen for the refineries spent hours and hours on the phone with plant personnel, since these custom-built orders took expertise on both ends.

The secretaries I managed were all experienced and needed little supervision. The Branch Manager, Serge Helfner, a Frenchman from World Trade, was constantly upset over what his secretary had said or didn't do that he should have done. We all had to put up with the guy. Even Frank, my boss, complained about the actions by this eccentric Branch Manager. I guess he was assigned to Baton Rouge because of the French influence in the state of Louisiana.

I had one problem desk, the card order function. Much of data processing in those days was still being done with cards. The IBM 360 was changing that, but we had many customers that still used all the card processing equipment. This person was not well organized and continued to make order errors. IBM required valid reasons to release someone. With Frank's guidance, I put the person on an improvement program. But it didn't work out, so the individual resigned. This was the most difficult task as a manager. You needed to believe and convince them that they would be more successful working in a job that was a better fit for their skills.

I had difficulty with the language, which was embarrassing at times. Once I kept calling a guy Mr. Hu Burt and it was "A Bear," spelled Hubert. I also had difficulty with the coffee. The machine coffee in the office came out in tiny cups so strong it was like syrup. I had to use tons of sugar in order to drink it. I stayed high on caffeine. The language was rough and a lot of cursing that did not set well with me. But we learned to enjoy Louisiana seafood, like raw oysters, oyster Po'boys and speckled trout.

Since Louisiana is known as a sportsman's paradise, I think the orders and movements guys decided to make a sportsman out of me. Gerald DeArmond was a fisherman. He had us over to his house for a speckled trout fish fry. They were the best fish we had ever eaten. After that, he had to take me fishing. One Saturday at 4 am Gerald, Frank and I were on our way to the Gulf of Mexico just off the Louisiana coast. We sat in that small boat all day and caught not a single fish of any kind.

Ken Reid was a hunter. He had to take me duck hunting. After investing in a hundred fifty dollar shotgun and forty dollar waders, I rode with him to Manchac, a peninsula on Lake Pontchartrain. We waded in swampy water up to our stomachs and not a single duck for us to shoot was seen, not that I could have hit it anyway. Ken did not give up. He planned a second duck hunt that was guaranteed to supply plenty of shooting opportunities. This time we went with some of his crazy Cajun friends. They loaded a boat to the point that the edge of the boat was just barely above the water, and we went barreling down the Chauplia River in total darkness with the temperature below freezing. I did some hard praying. When we reached their houseboat, sitting on the edge of the river, I expected it to at least be warm. Instead, I froze the rest of the night and all the next day. It turned out that night was the coldest ever recorded for that date in Louisiana's weather history. That morning we rode in a prow, which is a small boat that someone has to hold for you to sit down, and if you move it turns over. When we pulled the prow into the rack built into the duck blind, a sheet of ice formed on the sides of the prow. That was how cold it was. We saw some ducks, but none were close enough to shoot.

After the hunting and fishing failures, next came the annual overnight camping trip. This was for all the guys in administration in the office, about ten of us. We stayed in a cabin in a state park on a lake. Next day they were teaching me how to water ski, since I had never tried that before. I got the rope wrapped around my hand and after being pulled under water what seemed to be a hundred yards, the boat finally stopped, I came up and was saved from drowning. However, after Frank insisted, I went to the ER for an x-ray of my hand. Nothing was broken, but I was embarrassed explaining to everyone in the office how I happened to have a black and blue hand. After my experiences as a Louisiana Sportsman I decided if this is what they call paradise I wanted no part of it. No matter how hard they had tried to make a sportsman out of me, I learned I was not a winning candidate.

Even though I no longer had night school and homework, I put in enough hours working at IBM and commanding the Finance Unit in the Army Reserve, to find enough excuses not to attend church. My career ambitions were my priority. Kathy tried to get us involved in a church family. We attended Florida Boulevard Baptist a few times. Kathy even volunteered to teach a girl's class of teens. They were unruly and gave her such a bad time that she stopped. This is when she decided she was not sure she wanted to have a career teaching, as she once had planned.

I was leaving God out of my life, but God was still working out his plan for me. He was just letting me think that all my great decisions and successes were all my doing. With the way my life was going, I didn't feel any need to grow my faith. I knew I was saved from that experience years ago at the kitchen table when my Mother led me to accept Christ as my Savior. The next string of decisions I made resulted in the realization that I had been living only for myself and that I had to turn my life around and give priority to God's place in my life.

Chapter 23:

THE MIRACLE

⊰⊱

B y the end of 1968, IBM was growing at a record pace. Rumor had it that Corporate was about to separate out several entities in order to have smaller, more responsive units to service our growing base of customers. The Office Products operation was separated and formed into its own division from the Data Processing Division, and Field Engineering was separated into its own division. Administration management and staff were needed to support these two new divisions. After only eighteen months as an Administration Operations Manager I was offered the new Office Products Division Administration Manager position. Frank and I discussed the decision at length. It was a big deal to leave the Data Processing Division, the most successful and fastest growing business seldom experienced in the business world. Frank warned me that the management in the Office Products operation was not to be trusted. They were known for giving Administration Management a difficult time when they were held to the audit rules. A major responsibility for Administration was to enforce compliance with audit guidelines for doing business. IBM had recently been charged as a monopoly and was required by the Federal Government to abide by specific business guidelines. For example, an IBM salesperson could not disparage a competitor and their product. Sales management did not like or want to abide by these strict rules.

My desire to advance my career with this big promotion led me to go for it. I could handle the extra responsibility and workload. My IBM career was my priority. "Me" was my priority. I moved into the tiny office that had previously been a storage room. The IBM building was out of space due to the rapid growth. Construction of a new office was planned for the near future.

A meeting of all Office Products Division Administration Managers was announced for early May, 1969. It would be held in Lexington, KY, the home of the major manufacturing plant for the Office Products Division. We planned for Kathy and Lee, now 14 months old, to stay with my Mom and Dad while I attended the meeting. On Friday I planned to get a new set of tires for the car before leaving for Louisville the next morning. It was a 1966 Chrysler, and the original tires were now well worn. Placing IBM pressing matters first, I left work at 8 pm Friday night and did not have new tires for the car.

The car was loaded with all I needed for my trip, Kathy and Lee's suitcases, and Lee's play-bed. It was drizzling rain and the pavement on the Natchez Trace was slippery as I passed a slower car. The speed limit was 50, but I'm sure I was doing 60 to pass the car. Kathy was telling me to slow down. Suddenly the left rear tire blew, the car fish tailed and immediately swerved off the road. For a second it was airborne as it went over a small mound, and at that moment I saw the huge tree looming directly in my face. I turned the steering wheel, closed my eyes and cried, "Oh My Lord!" This was not the typical expression I may have said if surprised about something. For a split second, I felt that I was crying these words to Christ as He stood before me. The car did not turn, but the front wheels had turned; and when the car landed, the wheels turned the front away from the tree. The left rear door crashed into the tree. The crash stripped all the bark from the pine all the way around the tree. Kathy said later that she thought the car went all the way around the tree stripping the bark away. No way to know for certain. The first thing I remember was running back to the car. Lee and I were thrown completely out of the car. Kathy was hanging out the driver's door.

The miracle was before my eyes. If the car had crashed head-on into the tree, we would have all been killed. The motor would have been in our laps. The force of the impact bent the steel frame of the car and totaled it.

I do not remember hitting the ground. I remember running back to the car to help Kathy out. Her legs were up on the seat and her head was laying on the ground. Her forehead was bleeding, and she was in pain. I told her I could not see Lee. She said, "He is over there." I walked to him and picked him up. He was screaming. He had been asleep between us. His mouth was bloody. Just as I was picking him up and holding him, a couple was standing there. I handed him to them and asked them to take him to the Baptist Hospital in Jackson. Why I did that, I will never know. I knew Kathy's injuries were serious. I wanted a doctor to check Lee, but I knew we would need an ambulance for Kathy.

We were in a remote area, halfway between Jackson and Carthage. Someone had called Carthage for an ambulance. It took almost an hour for it to arrive. Meanwhile a crowd had stopped and gathered at the site. Everyone wanted to be helpful. We didn't know the extent of her head injury, so a nurse that had stopped kept Kathy talking. She complained that her arm was hurting really bad. It was broken in two places between her elbow and shoulder. It seemed the ambulance would never come. Getting her into the ambulance was painful. We learned later she had the multiple fractured arm, several broken ribs and the large laceration on her head. Nothing was life threatening, but all very painful.

As we were traveling in the ambulance, Kathy for the first time closed her eyes and became deathly quiet. I was afraid to check her pulse. I was afraid she had died. This was the first time since the accident that I prayed. My prayer to God was my repentance. If He would spare Kathy's life, I would turn my life around and live for Him. She explained later the reason she had closed her eyes was she had finally gotten relief from all the pain.

Upon arrival at the ER at Baptist Hospital, Jackson, the young couple I had sent to the hospital with Lee were standing there with him for over an hour, and he was still crying his heart out. The hospital had checked him for any life-threatening injuries but could not treat him because they were not his parents. I felt so terrible that I never got the young couples names. I also regret not keeping Lee with us. Lee had lost his three front teeth that were just coming in. He could no longer take his bottle because his mouth hurt so bad. He never used the bottle again. The first day Kathy was taken to him, he was so frightened because he did not recognize her with all the bandages on her. She was so upset. They wheeled me down to Lee's room, and he sat on my lap and ate ice cream. He relaxed and began to recover from the very traumatic experience he had suffered. He wore a plate for his front teeth until his adult teeth grew in.

God was taking care of me as always. Who was the on-duty ER doctor? None other than Dr. Thompson, my National Guard Battalion doctor. When he learned it was me and my family in the automobile wreck, he took charge. I did not have to do another thing. He got examinations going for all of us, and in a short time all our wounds were being treated. I could not be sure if I had any serious injuries. I had lacerations behind both knees. Both my ankles were bruised. We never determined what caused these injuries. My shoulder that opened the driver's door hurt. When they told me to breath deep and then hold my breath as they did a chest x-ray, I fainted.

By now, it was more than three hours past when we were to arrive at Louisville. Since my parents had not heard from us, they knew something terrible must have happened. I had to make the phone calls, but thankfully I was able to tell them that we were all going to be fine. I explained as best I could the injuries that we had. Both Mom and Dad and Mr. and Mrs. Rainer were at the hospital within two hours of when I called them. I was the humblest I had ever been. I explained it was completely my fault because I should have gotten new tires installed before we left on the trip.

I didn't tell them, but many, many times I have thought what would have happened to me if either Kathy or Lee had been killed. Just the thought of that is tough to live with. I still thank God for sparing our lives that day. I regret it took a terrible accident and caused suffering to my loved ones to get my life back into a closer relationship with Christ. I guess God knew what it would take. I had been humbled before God in a matter of seconds, and I was thankful beyond words for sparing our lives. It would have been certain death had we crashed head on into the tree.

Even though our injuries were not life threatening, our treatment required hospitalization. Kathy and Lee were dismissed after five days. I had to stay seven because one of my bruised ankles got infected and they would not release me until the infection was under control. Kathy and Lee stayed in the home of the McFarland's, one of the IBM Managers in the Jackson office, until I was dismissed from the hospital. Mrs. Rainer took a week off work from her factory job to go home with us and stay with Kathy and take care of Lee. With broken ribs and a broken arm, Kathy could not do anything for herself or Lee.

We were very fortunate to be able to hire Kathryn, a young sister of one of my employees in the office. Kathryn was still in high school. She was a wonderful caretaker. She did anything that Kathy and Lee needed. She worked all day cooking and cleaning. This allowed me to get back to work. When I got home from work, I did anything else that needed to be done.

It was about two months before Kathy was able to do light work. She had to sleep in a recliner for about a month. The ribs and arm healed nicely but took a long time and was very painful. She was such an unbelievably strong person and never once complained to me that all this was my fault. I felt so sorry for all her pain that I had caused. It would have served me right if she had never spoken to me again, and I could not have blamed her if she just decided to leave me for what I had done. God had given me this precious forgiving person as my wife. From now on I would do everything I could to take care of her.

When I went back to work, I was on crutches. My legs were both injured behind my knees and my ankles were both bruised. My legs drew up, so I had to do stretches each night to get them back to normal. Kathryn took Kathy to doctor appointments. The ribs and arm required x-rays to determine if they were healing correctly. Kathy was completely dependent on someone until the ribs were no longer painful. Kathy would stay in her recliner most all day. The neighborhood children would come over and play with Lee and sit and talk with Kathy. They made beautiful get-well cards for her and brought her candy. Kathy was a special person for the children, and they were disappointed when we moved away a couple of years later. As long as we lived there, the children always came around to visit Kathy and play with Lee. Later, when Steve was born, they had to visit and help out with entertaining Lee while Kathy took care of Steve.

The Baptist Hospital had given us the royal treatment. I am sure it was because Dr. Thompson had let everyone know that we were his special patients. We had fantastic rooms. Our parents came often for visits, and the IBM family made sure we had everything we needed. Even though we were in the hospital a week, the time flew by because each day was filled with visitors and hospital staff making sure we were comfortable. We were in the hospital, but not really sick, which was rather unique. Several IBM employees offered to have our folks stay with them when they came for visits. The care we received at the hospital and the IBM family caused me to think that one day I would like to be part of the IBM Office in Jackson once again. I didn't dream that it would become a reality in only two short years.

My life in Baton Rouge was not the same after the accident. IBM was no longer number one. My family was number one. It took time for Kathy to mend. I was home on time to relieve Kathryn. I did what was needed to help with Kathy and Lee. One of our neighbors, Mrs. Beaupre, had a son and daughter, age eight and six. They would take him to their house and entertain him. He loved them and they became his favorite playmates, even though they were much older.

Kathy's sister, Joyce, sent us a certificate for two free nights at a quaint little hotel in Miami. Since our two hour stay in Florida when we were on our two day honeymoon didn't count as ever visiting Florida, we decided to take the trip. We were actually celebrating that Kathy could finally leave the house for something other than a doctor's appointment. When we arrived in Miami, it was a very nice small hotel right on the ocean. We could hear the waves from inside our room. We learned there was a required high-pressure sales pitch attached to the free stay. This was our first experience of this kind, but was the only time we were convinced we should buy. Since it was in the back of our minds that we might someday retire to Florida, and since it was not very expensive, we decided to buy the lot they were selling in an undeveloped community. We paid monthly and had it paid off in about five years. About that time, we decided we would not plan to retire to Florida, so we put the lot up for sale. The realtor I contacted wrote back that she would put on her snake boots and go out and place a for sale sign on the property. It did finally sell, and we broke even. Today there is a beautiful community where we once owned a lot. Seems no matter where, if you wait long enough, land usually becomes valuable over time.

While at the hotel we both wanted to try swimming in the Atlantic, which neither of us had ever done. This is when God intervened in my life and let me live another day. We knew nothing about rip tide, and when one grabbed me, and me being the poor swimmer that I am, I felt I was gone. I prayed for God to save me, and at that moment my feet touched the ocean floor and I was able to spring my head above water. I thrashed my arms toward the shore. I have avoided swimming in the ocean since that experience. I learned that the ocean water even in Florida is too cold for me and that I was no match for a rip tide.

One other very significant event for our lives happened on the trip. Kathy got pregnant with Steve. The doctor had advised not to get pregnant for at least six months in order for her broken ribs to heal completely. However, I know because of many prayers by us and our parents, Kathy had a normal pregnancy without any complications, and we were blessed with another fine boy on June 3, 1970.

While living in Baton Rouge, Kathy and I had many traumatic experiences. However, we were granted the most wonderful blessings that a couple can experience. Both of our children, Lee and Steve, were born at Woman's Hospital in Baton Rouge. Our two boys turned out to be the greatest blessing to us the rest of our lives. Neither of them have ever given us any trouble of any kind. They live their lives today honoring us and God, living Christ centered lives and working for His kingdom on this earth. Parents cannot ask for a blessing any greater.

Chapter 24:

THE JACKSON MISSISSIPPI YEARS

⟫⟨

After the catastrophic event in the Spring of 1969, the remainder of that year was a time for reflection and restart. Kathy had injuries that took a long time to mend. I was feeling so guilty that I did everything I could to assist in getting her well. Even though Kathryn was a great help and companion for her during the day while I was at work, when I got home there was plenty for me to do. I was a changed person after the wreck. My family became my priority. All I could think about was how thankful I was that neither Kathy nor Lee were killed or had permanent debilitating injuries. I was now a devoted family man. No more hunting, fishing and outings trying to become a Louisiana Sportsman. I did my job as Administration Manager, but IBM was no longer my number one priority. I was Commander of a small Finance Reserve Unit. I didn't let it take much of my time, and it gave me the opportunity to continue my career in the National Guard and now the Reserves.

My most difficult management task was having to evaluate the performance of an employee and rate him or her unsatisfactory. IBM required a formal improvement program before they could be released. I had to work through two more of these situations in Baton Rouge. In both cases the employee resigned when they understood they would be more successful in another line of work. I lost one good employee that confided in me that she was having an affair with the married Customer Engineering Branch Manager, whom she was supporting in her job. She was also married and seemed to not blame him for the situation. I told her if she continued this and it was reported, he would be fired. She later resigned.

In the Spring of 1971, Mr. Rainer boarded the bus in Newton bound for Columbus, GA to visit his two brothers. While there he became very ill. They took him to the hospital, where he was diagnosed with lung cancer. He had smoked since he was a teenager. He underwent major surgery to remove one lung, and it had spread to the other lung. There was little hope that he could live much longer. We visited him once while he was still hospitalized in GA. As soon as he was able to travel, they brought him to his home in Newton.

Again God was ever present directing our lives, because the Administration Manager's job in Jackson, MS, became open. I contacted my District Manager and asked if I could be considered for the position. He said if the Branch Manager agreed to interview me and if he approved me for the job, then I could be transferred to the Jackson office. I interviewed and was accepted by the Branch Manager. I know that my desire for us to be near our folks, especially at this time with the condition of Mr. Rainer, had some influence toward approving my request to transfer. I am sure he would have liked to interview other candidates he had in mind. We worked well together for many years.

After quickly finding a new home almost completely finished, we moved in May, 1971 to 1142 Woodfield Drive, our home for the next 9 years. It was located in North Jackson, in a new development with many young families. Lee and Steve always had loads of play mates the entire time we lived there. They played well with everyone and never created problems for us. Our large lot backed up to an open field and some wooded area. They had days and days of freedom playing with neighborhood children and roaming the entire neighborhood. In those days, we didn't worry that any harm would come to them in our safe community.

When we moved, Lee was two and a half and Steve eleven months old. They were both excited that we had to sleep on the carpeted bedroom floor our first night in our new home. The movers did not arrive until the next day. It was only a three bedroom, so the boys shared a room and we used the remaining bedroom as a guest room. They put up with each other very well. When Lee started to school, he would teach Steve what he learned in school that day. As they got older and both were in school, they would have school with the Skipper brothers across the street who were three and four years younger.

Kathy did most of the work and gets all the credit for our two boys to be the outstanding men that they have become. The only thing I can think of which I did that they appreciated was to build a little fort-like addition onto my lawnmower storage shed. They helped me build it and they spent many enjoyable hours playing in and out of the fort, pretending it was the real thing.

Lee and Steve's Friends Loved Playing in the Fort

Kathy spent some time with her Dad after he returned to Newton. She could not give up on him. She tried hard to get him to eat and get out of bed, hoping he could gain strength and recover. Mr. Rainer had given up and wanted to go to his heavenly reward. Kathy regretted pushing her Dad so hard, and the day she was planning to return and make it up to him, we got the call that he had passed away at the age of 66. He had lived his entire life in Newton. He was a painter, carpenter and wallpaper hanger. He was the best domino player and bream fisherman in Newton. I had many enjoyable fishing trips with him and his partner, A. B. Amos, the best attorney in town. They never missed a Saturday fishing at the lake at Roosevelt State Park in Morton, MS. Many times, they also fished a day during the week. Mr. Rainer knew everyone in Newton and had many friends. They all came to his funeral. The large First Baptist Church where Kathy and I were married was overflowing. I regret that the boys were not old enough to get to know and remember their fun loving, always happy Pappy Rainer.

After Mr. Rainer's death, we were more and more thankful that we were living near our folks, especially Mrs. Rainer, who was now living alone, but still working at the pants factory. We had many visits together with our parents on all the holidays and birthdays. We were very blessed to have the boys growing up with and getting to know their grandparents. To this day, they try to follow in their footsteps to live the Christian example their grandparents lived out during their lifetimes.

Mom and Dad's 50th Wedding Anniversary Reception

One very special occasion was Mom and Dad's 50th Wedding Anniversary on July 4th, 1979. Their marriage ceremony was held at the preacher's home and very informal. Carey and I planned to honor their love and devotion to each other and their love for us with a reception at Evergreen Baptist Church on a Sunday afternoon. Some of the ladies of the church took charge and organized a wonderful reception for them, to include Mom and Dad's nieces as servers for the cake and punch. They made sure all the church family and Mom and Dad's relatives were invited for the time of fellowship. Carey's and my families stood in the reception line with Mom and Dad as their church family and relatives honored them with their well wishes of congratulations. It was such an honor to stand with them and see the outpouring of love from their church family and relatives. The boys were all decked out in their Sunday suits. I know at their young age they were amazed at the number of people that came to honor their grandparents. This I am sure made a lasting impression of just how important a church family and family members are to one's life.

All that was happening in the United States in the 70's was very stressful and discouraging to say the least. Our country seemed to be torn apart by many actions of protesting the "status quo." The war in Vietnam, Civil Rights violence, rioting as a result of the assassination of Dr. Martin Luther King Jr, the sexual revolution and the racial divisions and strife resulting from all the changes the South and nation faced as a result of the Civil Rights Act. A good example was school busing. Children and teachers were required to move to schools located away from their community schools in order to accomplish desegregation.

I was very thankful that the Jackson office did not have any major personnel issues related to the many crises occurring across the United States and world. Even the energy shortage did not impact MS. I don't recall many long lines at the gas pump during that time. We were all impacted by inflation which was out of control. However, IBM addressed it by giving everyone two raises in the same year instead of the normal one raise.

One distraction my staff presented that took my valuable time was the issue of divorces. At one time there were three happening within my staff. I spent time counseling for which I had no experience or qualification to help. It is very frustrating when a manager cannot help solve an employee's problem. One night, an employee awoke us in the wee hours of the morning at our door, very drunk, asking to stay with us. His wife had locked him out of his house. We sat and drank coffee at our kitchen table until daybreak.

On top of everything else, the Watergate Investigation was adding to the divisions across the nation. I had been a Republican ever since Ronald Reagan made his TV speech for Barry Goldwater. Needless to say, I stood by Nixon until the exposure of the White House tapes. I recall reading about Chuck Colson, the hatchet man for Nixon, being sent to prison for his actions as White House counsel. I would never have dreamed that one day we would come to know him personally and be a part of Prison Fellowship, the organization he founded as a result of being in prison. God has His plan if we just sit tight and let Him implement it.

The Jackson office personnel were dedicated to their jobs and they were thankful to be working for just about the best company in the world, so they kept personal feelings about politics, religion, civil rights and any controversial subjects to themselves. That's the way I operated, and I think most all of us did. The outside world had many distractions, but inside the IBM operation, we were concentrating on doing a good job. IBM was so successful that we were striving, as they say, to keep our heads above the water. My staff did such a great job that we were awarded the Regional Office of the year in 1972 and 1975. The award is based on various measurements for the various administrative functions, and we competed with the other ten offices in our district. The award entitled me to attend the IBM Means Service Conference in Fort Lauderdale in 1972 and Montreal in 1975. After the conference in Montreal, Kathy flew up and we did a road trip to Quebec City.

I also had the opportunity to attend our annual Administration Managers' meetings. These were recognition and motivational meetings for managers held at nice resorts. The meetings were always relaxing and enjoyable and included site seeing trips. One I remember vividly, because I have been afraid of heights since, was going up in the Arch in St. Louis. I had Kathy join me at Lake of the Ozarks after the conference we had there. Mrs. Rainer was staying with the boys at our home. While we were away, a little dog, that had come to our house and we adopted, got run over and killed. So Kathy and I came home with Heidi, a registered German schnauzer puppy. Heidi was their wonderful pet for many years. She lived to be 16 years old. Thankfully, the boys were away at college when she died, so Kathy and I buried her in our back yard. She was a terrific pet but liked to stray away from home at any opportunity. Once, in Jackson, she went missing for several days and turned up across an interstate and river 10 miles away in south Jackson. We believe she had to have been taken there. In New Jersey, she always went to the fire station and they would bring her back home.

Chapter 25:

FINALLY A CHURCH FAMILY

⋈

We had joined the Woodland Hills Baptist Church in the Spring of 1971, when we first moved to Jackson. For the first time in our married life we became faithful and enjoyed the fellowship of a church family. Our neighbors B and Billie Skipper had invited us to attend. It was again God preparing the way for our lives, because the church had a Christian School; and later, as Lee and Steve started to public school, it became necessary to have them attend Woodland Hills because of the busing issues with the public schools. We first tried the public schools. Lee would come home crying because of all the loud and disruptive children, even bullying that the teacher had little control over. His bus ride was too frightening to him. When we moved them to Woodland Hills, they had to do extra work to catch up. The learning environment there was very disciplined, and all the teaching was to get learning results. There were no easy grades. This turned out to be a great blessing when we moved to New Jersey and they attended public school. They were up to par with the excellent public schools in the affluent community of Wyckoff.

It was at Woodland Hills that Kathy and I realized we needed to grow our faith and set a Christian example for our boys, just as our parents had done for us. These years at Woodland Hills got us back on track to be faithful in our attendance, giving and participation in the church family. The boys were grounded in the Christian faith, attending Sunday School Bible Study and attending the Christian school. As they grew older, they understood their sinful nature and their need for accepting Christ as their Savior. Lee was attending a revival service at another church with his Cub Scout leader and her son when he felt led to go down and accept Christ during the invitation. We were surprised but rejoiced with him over his decision. He then joined the Woodland Hills Baptist Church.

My participation in church was attending and supporting financially. I was not asked nor did I volunteer to take any responsible duties. I was away once a month for National Guard duties. One year we trained twice a month preparing for deployment to Vietnam. Kathy and the boys were happy to spend those weekends with Mrs. Rainer while I was attending National Guard duty in Newton. We also visited my parents for all holidays and birthdays. Mrs. Rainer and my parents visited us often, for it was an easy trip for them. These were the most wonderful times of our lives, being with loved ones on special occasions. They were able to see our boys growing up, and more importantly our boys saw the love of Christ exemplified in their lives and their love and participation in a church family.

While living in Jackson we took several short vacation trips. One to Disney World, which the boys loved. A few days at a Florida beach. We didn't need any better vacation time than spending time with our parents and grandparents. The boys enjoyed all the exploring at our farm in Louisville, fishing in Mrs. Rainer's catfish pond and walking to downtown Newton on the railroad track. We even went hunting once on our farm.

Our years in Jackson, if not the best years of our lives, were very nearly the best. We were very, very blessed during these years. We can rest assured that God planned for us to be there. Kathy had a number of years as a stay at home Mom before the boys started to school. She and the neighbor, Billie, and her two boys shared many hours in activities for the children. There were swim lessons, playgrounds and parks to visit, church activities and neighborhood birthday parties. These years were very critical for proper development of the two sets of boys. All four of them have grown up to be successful in their professional calling and have stayed focused in their Christian walk. They grew up in families filled with love for them by both their parents and grandparents. In addition, they were surrounded by love from their Christian church family. Knowing this about my life and our children's lives, when I heard our pastor recently coin the phrase "This Beautiful Thing Called Church," I knew I needed to title my memories just that. Because my first church family and those after it have brought me to where I am today in my faith and walk with God. Hallelujah and Amen. During these years I was busy earning a living and had less time with the boys than Kathy. That is why I know she and God get all the credit for our two outstanding sons.

Chapter 26:

THE MAKING OF A CERTIFIED PUBLIC ACCOUNTANT

><|<

I n 1975, when Steve started kindergarten and Lee was in second grade, Kathy began her long awaited career goal of getting her college degree. She had always planned to be a teacher. We discussed other careers that she believed she would enjoy, and settled on a degree in Accounting. She had always excelled in all of her studies. She enrolled at Belhaven, a private Presbyterian University near our home. She also took some night courses at the University Center that offered courses from both Mississippi State and Ole Miss. In only two year she earned her degree. She graduated with honors. My parents, her mother and our boys, all decked out in our Sunday best, were in attendance. We were more than proud of our wife, mother and daughter. It was an outside ceremony on a beautiful sunshiny day. It had been eighteen years since she graduated from high school. It was a very happy day, and I was especially proud of her because I knew how much it meant to her and how hard she had worked. I had helped out some with the house duties, but she had kept everything going at home in addition to her school work. To honor her accomplishment, we splurged and bought her a new 77 Olds Cutlass Supreme, two door hard-top.

She landed a job working part time for a CPA. Part time because she could pick the boys up from school. She always made sure she had part time work until the boys were older and responsible enough to be home alone after school. After working a short time for the CPA, with his encouragement, she set her goal to study for the CPA exam. I also encouraged her for I knew she was capable. You have to pass at least two parts of a four part exam. She thought she passed all four parts on her first try. She had not passed any and was very discouraged. You are not told your scores so you cannot know how close you came on each part. We decided she needed to take the CPA Review course before her second try. The review course was available in Memphis or New Orleans on six weekends. We traveled to the course and I entertained the boys while Kathy was in class. We did site seeing in the two cities. I got in some quality time with just me and the boys. They were young enough that they were never bored with all the places we got to see.

In New Orleans we visited the Super Dome and the French Quarter. I ran a stop sign in the French Quarter and a speeding van hit the right front of Kathy's new Cutlass. We were all very thankful that no one was hurt. The van was almost able to stop before impact. However, the police gave me a real scare. Since I was from out of state, had run a stop sign resulting in a wreck, and since it was Sunday, I would have to be held in jail until Monday to appear before a Judge. I carefully and politely explained our situation. The boys were cryiing. I had no way to contact Kathy, and even if I could have, she had no way to come pick up the boys. The kind man driving the van that hit us convinced the policeman to not give us a ticket. He explained he was traveling too fast or he would have been able to stop. In fact, he skidded and was almost stopped before he hit us. They all felt sorry for us and we were so thankful there was no ticket and no jail time. We did not return to the French Quarter. We stayed close to Kathy's building where she was attending class trying to come up with the best excuse for wrecking her new car.

The review course worked, because the next time she took the exam, she passed two parts which meant she could pass the other two parts one at a time. But, she passed both parts the next time she sat for the exam. In March, 1981, we celebrated Kathy's outstanding accomplishment of earning the coveted title of Certified Public Accountant.

Chapter 27:

THE DEBACLE OF A SECOND LINE MANAGER

➤|◄

W ith the rapid growth of IBM and the added responsibility for the Administration Manager to implement the provisions of the Civil Rights Law, in just a few years my staff had grown to require two Operation Managers that reported to me. My promotion to second line management turned out to not be a good thing. Instead of me managing the people, I had to rely on these two first line managers for the day to day dealing with the employees.

I had hired minorities at every opportunity, and I also now had a minority first line manager, Jerry. In 1979 we were working together on the salary plan for his employees for the coming year. The Regional Office rejected one of the raises that we submitted, and that raise happened to be for a minority. Unknown to me, Jerry had told the employee about the planned raise before it was approved or in this case, disapproved. As a result, the employee wrote a speak up. A speak up was the open-door policy in IBM. Each speak up was investigated at length by interviewing all parties involved, and a determination was made if the employee had been wronged. If so, it would be corrected, and action taken to prevent future errors like the one made. Many times, it resulted in discipline of the manager that caused the error. In my interview with the investigator, I confirmed that the Regional Office had denied the raise that we had submitted, even though, to no avail, I tried to convince the Regional Administration Manager to approve the raise. Of course the employee got the raise she was told she would get. I was faulted for my not being aware the employee was told by her manager she would get the raise before it was approved. Jerry was not faulted because he was a first line manager that was anxious to let his employee know that she was getting a raise. I believe he was not faulted because he was a minority. My Branch Manager and my Regional Manager were not pleased with how I had failed to enforce non-communication of the planned raise before it was approved. It was really ironic that I had worked so hard to increase minority representation on my staff that these two minorities were the cause for my situation. I was always very truthful in all my dealings in IBM, so I had told it exactly as it happened. I really didn't believe it was all my fault, but I understood the desire not to penalize an inexperienced first line manager.

It was determined that I would need to relocate and probably accept a demotion to first line management. For a month, my Regional Manager made attempts to get me a position, offering me a first line manager position in Memphis which I declined. Then he offered me a first line manager position at the Lexington Plant, managing a pool of secretaries. Again, I declined. Finally, he offered me a position in the Regional Office in Kansas City, and I would not be demoted. It would be at my same level, second line manager. I believed this was my best option, and I would not be impacted financially.

From Thanksgiving, 1979 to May 1980 was the most difficult six months of my IBM career. Just before the Thanksgiving holiday, the Jackson Branch Manager announced my assignment to the Kansas City Regional Office. My acceptance speech was as upbeat as I could make it. I emphasized how much I had enjoyed

154

my time in the Jackson office and how much I appreciated the great job they had done for me. We were looking forward to my Kansas City assignment, which was not being quite truthful, but what could I say.

Bill Schaper, my new boss, recommended I take Thanksgiving week off and report to Kansas City on Monday, the last week in November. It was cold, damp and dreary weather that matched my mood. I was home alone. Kathy was working and the boys were in school. I built a fire in the fireplace, and Heidi and I would sit by the fire. After two days, I decided I had to do something. Mrs. Rainer's porch needed painting, and I needed to break the news to her about us having to leave Jackson, so I took off for Newton and worked two days painting the porch. Mrs. Rainer was sad we would be moving, but said she understood why I needed to stay with IBM. We were planning to go to my folks for Thanksgiving, so we took Mrs. Rainer with us. It was a big shock for my folks that we would be moving and put a somber mood for our Thanksgiving. All of us have faith in God and believe He has a plan for our lives. That strong faith makes a big difference when we face critical decisions and changes in our situation. We pray for God's guidance as we move forward into the unknown.

When I reported to Kansas City, there was no assigned responsibility. I was given various tasks, including performing self-audits for branches in the Region. These audits were designed to prepare a branch office for the dreaded and real corporate audits. Administration Management were responsible for satisfactory audits of their branch. In my years as manager in the branch office, I always received very satisfactory audits.

This assignment meant not only traveling from Jackson to Kansas City every Sunday afternoon and return on Friday afternoon, but also traveling to the branch office for the onsite audits. Frankly, this was just too much travel. Winter was very snowy that year in Kansas and Missouri. One Friday it was snowing so hard in Kansas City that the plane was late, and I didn't make it home until after midnight. Once, on a trip to Jefferson City, Missouri for an audit, the small plane took off in a blinding snowstorm. I was stupid to board the plane. The pilot had to follow the highway at a very low altitude in order to find his way to Jefferson City. I prayed hard all the way and promised God I would never take such a risk again.

So I was somewhat relieved when an assignment at Office Products Division Headquarters became available. I was assigned to work on a Task Force Team formed to determine the cause and fix problems with one of the critical billing systems for Administration. I would now commute to Montvale, NJ, every two weeks for the duration of the Task Force. It was not the assignment I would have asked for, but it did mean that I could devote my skills to a worthwhile assignment. I was a good fit for this assignment because I once performed the process desk in the Branch Office for this critical billing file. Exposure to Division Headquarters would be good for my IBM future, especially if I did a good job on the Task Force.

As the Task Force for resolving the system billing problems wound down at the end of April, 1980, I was about to be released back to the Kansas City Regional Office. Here again God opened a door that would present the greatest challenge and the hardest decision I had ever faced. A System Analyst position in Office Products Division Headquarters had opened up, and the Manager I had worked for on the Task Force asked me if I would be interested in the position. Of course I expressed interest. However, before I could give my answer, I would need to discuss this major change with my family during the upcoming weekend. Moving to New Jersey had never been one of my career objectives.

The following weekend, Kathy and I prayed, cried and listed every pro and con we could think of that needed to be given consideration before we took this major upheaval of our lives. We were concerned for the boys, for they loved Woodland Hills and were getting a well-rounded Christian education. We had only been in Kathy's new home of her dreams, that she had designed, less than a year. Since we had lived in Jackson many years, we would be leaving our many friends. And of course, it felt like we would be a million miles away from our folks.

I even suggested I could resign from IBM and maybe get back into Retail Management. I was still young enough to embark on a new career. Kathy was well on her way to becoming a CPA. We didn't tell the boys we were moving. I think we took them out to eat and asked them what they thought about us moving to New Jersey. They didn't seem to be so upset or concerned as we thought they would be. It could be that I had been gone so much that this would mean I would be back living with them.

After talking and talking, I will never forget, Kathy and I were in our bedroom, sitting on the edge of the bed, and I hugged Kathy and we both cried. We almost decided not to take the job, but I finally realized it would be foolish to throw away seventeen years of a fantastic IBM career. Kathy had never questioned any decision I made regarding my career. I believe she loved and believed in IBM as much as I did. We sat right there on the edge of the bed and decided we would move to New Jersey. Again, God was working His will in our lives, for this move was a major turning point in all of our lives.

Chapter 28:

THE NEW JERSEY EXPERIENCE

>⊱⊰

The first week of July 1980, we made the rounds to say goodbye to our parents. It would be six long months before we would come for a visit to see them at Christmas. After moving from Mississippi, we always used two weeks in July and two weeks at Christmas for our vacations. We stayed in motels and took extra time seeing sights that interested the boys. They were always great travelers and some of my fondest memories were our times together in our car for the long trip. We would sing and listen to country radio. We especially liked "Alabama". During this period they were having number one hits after another.

One year we had a CB radio when it was popular, but the trucker language was so bad we decided it was not a good thing to have. The only time anything was stolen from our car was on a trip to Niagara Falls. They took only the CB radio. I think God was saying we should not have the thing.

It was indeed sad for us and our folks that we were moving so far away. We talked by phone weekly and wrote letters letting them know how we were doing and telling them all the things we were getting to do and see. The first time that Mom and Dad ever flew was when we lived in New Jersey. Carey arranged for them to fly to Denver, where he and his wife Toni lived. From there, they put Mom and Dad on a plane for Newark, NJ. We met their flight, and they stayed a few days with us. We showed them where I worked and our church and the town of Wyckoff. We even took them sightseeing in New York City. Dad could not stop talking about the size of the buildings and the number of people and cars everywhere. Being from a small town where there is only four two story buildings, did put New York in a very different perspective. I know they were happy to learn we had joined and were participating in a Baptist Church.

On our trips back home, we attended Kathy's family reunion held each year the first Saturday after the fourth of July. This was a great blessing for us to be with them even if for only a short time. The Livingston's had only one reunion, which was the only time our boys were able to meet all of Dad's brothers and many of my first cousins.

On our trip to our new home in New Jersey we made it a real vacation time. We stopped in Tennessee and toured Lookout Mountain and Rock City. After all the years of seeing "See Rock City" painted on the sides of barns, we finally actually saw Rock City. We toured Natural Bridge, Virginia and Lexington, Virginia and the Pennsylvania Amish Country. Driving into New Jersey, I was not sure how to get to Wyckoff. I saw an exit from the freeway that had an arrow for New York City. I said oh no, we have gone too far, so I made the next exit, then proceeded to get lost. After a while, I finally stopped and asked how to get to Wyckoff. I had not gone too far. The New York arrow just meant to follow that way if you wanted to go to New York City. I know Kathy and the boys wondered how we would survive in New Jersey if I was not even able to find our town.

Lee and Steve Ready to Leave for New Jersey

We wanted to live in Wyckoff because our friends, Glen and Glenda Boulton from Mississippi, lived in Wyckoff. Glen was a CE Manager in Jackson when I worked on the maintenance desk. We became pals with them. They were both from the tiny community, Rose Hill, about fifteen miles from Newton. It was really out in the country. We would get together on weekends and cook Chef Boyardee pizza. Often we would eat three of them.

Wyckoff was a bedroom community for commuters into the city. It was an affluent town, and the home prices were almost double what we owned in Mississippi. Again, God provided for us financially. When we moved to Jackson in 1971, I had the desire to own some farmland. I had always had as a goal to be a businessman and own a cattle farm. The job I had did not leave time for me to own cattle. I kept reading ads in the paper for land for sale. I spotted a tree farm for sale in the county next door, Madison County. I thought I could manage a tree farm along with the job

I had at IBM. So, in 1971, my brother and I purchased a hundred and fifty acres tree farm for forty three thousand dollars. We did not spend any cash. We both had IBM stock that we put up as collateral for the loan. During the next eight years the rate of inflation doubled the value of the farm. In addition, during those eight years we sold timber worth what we paid for the farm. We paid off our loans and owned the tree farm debt free.

The farm had an old, old house built in the 1800's. It was falling down. It was built with hewed out logs with stucco between them. Some friends of ours later moved the house, restored it and it is now on the National Register. Mine and Carey's names are on the deed history as the last owners. We could not believe it when we saw the house after it was restored. Behind the house was a huge fig tree that had wonderful figs each year. We made fig preserves just like my Grandmother Livingston had when I was growing up.

I made many trips to check on the tree farm, especially when we were having timber harvested. I bought a small chainsaw and cut wood for our wood burning fireplace. In retrospect I should not have been alone in the isolated forest using a chainsaw. Once, I took Lee with me when he was only four years old. I decided to change oil in my pickup while parked in the woods. Having never performed this task before on this pickup, I crawled under the truck and mistakenly drained the transmission fluid. All the hot fluid spilled out before I managed to get the plug screwed back. Lee and I then had to walk two miles in the summer humid heat to a country store for transmission fluid. Poor Lee was too small to walk that far. I had to carry him part of the way. Lee had an exciting story to tell about being stranded in the woods with Dad. Then, to my embarrassment, I would have to explain how it came about.

Our neighbors, Sim and Sharon, were having a house built in a new development. It had a club house, swimming pool, fishing lake and lots of open spaces that the boys could enjoy. The boys at this time needed separate bedrooms, so we contracted with the same builder to build a custom home. Kathy had every room and every cabinet she wanted. We were a bit extravagant and needed some extra cash to cover the down payment for our new home. After discussing with my brother, we decided we would see if we could find a buyer for the tree farm. Immediately, Georgia Pacific, a huge lumber industry company, wanted to buy the farm and would pay a hundred fifty thousand dollars. They would pay us in three equal installments over three years plus interest. This was a huge profit for us. This is how we were able to afford a house in the affluent town of Wyckoff.

God knew well before we did that we were going to need this money for the next move in His plan for our life. We always supported our church and other worthwhile charities. We never lived beyond our means. I was raised to "waste not want not." Kathy was always supportive of being reasonable with our spending. We always discussed and agreed on big ticket items. Like me, she was raised in a family that had only the bare necessities. Our parents did not live in debt. All of our financial gains came when there was a need. I believe if we are trying to live in God's will He is caring for not only our spiritual needs but also our physical needs.

New Jersey was a great educational experience for us all. Whatever we had feared actually did not exist. The people as a whole were friendly, good neighbors and enjoyable to know. The small church we found had some displaced Southerners like us, so our closest friends were from the South. My work was rewarding. The pay was excellent. IBM had various salary areas across the country based on cost of living. I was coming from the lowest to the highest area. My increases were geared to catching me up to the high area. My field experience was good for solving system issues and problems for the end users. Soon I was working on a new development project. Tony Alexander and I took a project for Rental Real Time Processing from start to finish. This resulted in automation of the last manual administrative operation in the field. Working directly with the programmers gave me valuable system development experience that would enhance my future opportunities.

Our first six months were really, really hard on Lee and Steve. They were age twelve and ten, had no friends except the two daughters of Glen and Glenda. They were about the same ages. But at Steve and Lee's ages, girls were not their favorite playmates. Anyway, Susan and Mimi already had friends to play with.

Until school started, Mom kept them busy. Our house had a half-finished basement, so they used it for their games and pretend characters. Mom took them to movies. They saw Star Wars three times. They could walk to downtown Wyckoff. It had one grocery store, Grand Union, one hardware and a Five and Dime very much like the one I managed in Forest, MS. They could walk to Friendly's, a burger and ice cream restaurant. Somehow they made it until school started. I know they were nervous about a new school but wanted to meet and make new friends. Steve could walk through the woods behind our house to his Elementary School. Lee rode a school bus two miles to his Middle School. Steve did really well adjusting to his new school. One of the Boulton daughters, Mimi, was in his class. She was popular so she welcomed Steve into her circle of friends. The following year he was elected President of his class. I don't think he ran for the office. I think Mimi got him elected. I believe that is the only elective office Steve has had. He was not into that. The school had a good music program, and Steve took guitar and sort of learned to play it.

Lee didn't fare so well the first few months. One or two ridiculed him, made fun of his southern accent and bullied him when no one was watching. Lee would not be intimidated. He stood proud of his Southern heritage. One day after school he made an appointment with the major bully to meet in the woods behind our house. The kid was bigger than Lee. The bully had a guy with him. The bully got in the first hard blow to Lee's face, knocking off his glasses and breaking them. That stopped the fight. Lee came home with broken glasses and a bruised and bloody face. Kathy was so sympathetic and calm. When I got home, I was so upset. I wanted to go to the bully's house and call his Dad out. Thankfully, I was talked out of that or we may have had two bloody faces. Word about the fight got to the teachers. The boys had to apologize to each other. Lee had no more problems. He may have lost the fight, but he gained respect for standing up to the bully.

Lee became good friends with John Camper at school and in the youth group at Bergen Baptist. John was into football and was built for it. Lee went out but didn't get to play much. He was just not quite big enough. He and John did weights. Lee became very strong. Lee always gave it his best. One cold evening after work I was watching football practice. Two big lineman hit Lee at the same time and he went out cold, flat on his back. It scared me. His breath was knocked out, but he was up in a minute. Later in Virginia, Lee also went out for football at James Madison High. His great friend, Scott Zimmerman, was a good player. He encouraged Lee. Again, Lee was just not quite big enough to get to play very much. We saw him once tackle the ball carrier, cause a fumble and recover it. That was very exciting, and we were so glad we got to see it since he didn't get to play very much. Once Lee fractured a rib in practice. He didn't say anything to anyone at first. After two days he finally got an X-ray and sure enough he had a rib fracture. Lee was determined and proved he was as tough as any of the other players. I know how painful rib fractures can be because of Kathy's fractures suffered in our car wreck. Even though Lee was never able to play much, the experience of football was a worthwhile learning experience. He has grown to be the most caring and participating father for his children. Much better than I ever was. He and his wife, Kris, have done an unbelievable job caring for their son, Daniel, who has a disability.

I am thankful we moved to New Jersey, especially for the boys. The New Jersey public schools were excellent. The teachers were innovative and required much work. The boys did well in their studies in both New Jersey and Virginia. Both were accepted at prestigious universities. It was the greatest of blessing to us that both Lee and Steve were good students, did well in college, and remained steadfast in their faith in God. Both were active in InterVarsity. They both have Christian friends from InterVarsity that they have maintained over many years.

A few weeks after we moved into our home in New Jersey, we rode down the street a few blocks from our house and located a Baptist church listed in the phone book. This was God's plan for us in motion. The next Sunday when we attended, it seemed like we were back home. They were friendly and welcomed us. One family, the Campers, were from Virginia Beach. The Youth Director, Tina White, was from Texas. She worked for JC Penny in their Corporate Office in New York City. The Pastor was from Texas. Tina had activities planned for the youth every weekend. Kathy and I were asked to serve. Kathy joined the choir led by Mrs. Camper, the most talented musician we had ever met. I was asked to be a Deacon. I told the Pastor I did not feel qualified because I smoked. He said we will help you stop. I knew I was needed. I also knew the example you needed to live in order to qualify to serve as a Deacon. My Dad had served as a Deacon for many years. I later served in a large church, Columbia Baptist in Virginia. The Pastor asked me to serve in our current church, Spring Hill, but I declined because Kathy had begun to have dementia issues and I could not leave her alone.

As a Deacon, I participated in a miracle at Bergen Baptist. The Pastor and Deacons prayed over his wife for healing of a tumor and it disappeared. I had always believed in prayer but had not witnessed a miracle like this. I had called on the Lord as our car was headed straight to a tree and the car turned, slamming the back rear door into the tree, which saved our lives. I know that was also a miracle from God.

When the Pastor accepted a call from a church in Texas, I was asked to chair a Search Committee for a new Pastor. I didn't feel qualified, but God lead me to a wonderful Pastor, Jack Mercer. I didn't know where to start, so I contacted the Baptist Association for New Jersey and New York combined. There were so few Baptist Churches, the association covered two states. One applicant stood out. Jack was working on his PhD at Princeton. He was from Kentucky. He agreed to serve as an interim until we found a permanent pastor. After a few weeks, the church called him to be our permanent pastor. He was an excellent pastor and led the growth of the church for many years. He initiated a building program, and we built a beautiful new building for worship. Our previous building was a very old cinder block building, cold and leaky.

The New Bergen Baptist Church

Jack Mercer's leadership took a small church in New Jersey and made it a great witness for Christ. Tina White's leadership of the youth helped our youth stay centered in their Christian walk. Her influence at this season of their lives helped our boys grow stronger in their faith. Their Christian friends gave them the peer associations that are so very important for example and accountability. We are thankful for Tina, and we still keep in touch over these many years. She later married and now lives back in her home state of Texas.

God had arranged for the right people at this place and this time to carry on His Kingdom work here on earth. The church was small, and when we had a pot luck lunch, we were like a large family. Our fellowship was humble, thankful for each other and sincere. When our current Pastor at Spring Hill titled one of his sermons "This Beautiful Thing Called Church," I was reminded of the beautiful church family at Bergen Baptist.

Our neighbor across the street was a banker executive that commuted by train every day to the city. One Saturday afternoon, he and his wife invited us to go to Madison Square Garden. We would see the Barnum and Bailey Circus. They had box seats, so it was quite a treat. His driving in the city was rather embarrassing. His swearing at every car in front of us covered the entire swear dictionary. I worried that the boys would start using some of these new words.

Kathy did not work summers. She worked part time with a two partner CPA firm. The two partners did not get along well. One other employee in the office did not talk very much. I know that Kathy brought some cheerfulness into their office. They really appreciated her. One of the partners gave her a great recommendation when she applied for a job in Virginia.

During our years in New Jersey, I was always interested in a move back South, in order for us to be closer to our parents. I kept my manager aware of my favorite locations, but nothing ever came available. I interviewed to be an Internal Auditor stationed in Atlanta. I would have gotten the job, but I found out later my former manager in Kansas City did not give me a favorable recommendation. I was upset of course.

I know now that God shut the door on my desire and plan but opened the door to a much better opportunity. IBM in the early eighties was having difficulties. Competition was giving IBM fits with the Personal Computer. The PC was replacing the entire line of IBM Office Products. IBM had gotten too big to react rapidly to the changing needs of the customer. The smaller, less expensive PC manufactures were winning the day. The first action by IBM to eliminate the Office Products Division was to consolidate the processing systems into one. So the Office Products System would be moved to Bethesda, MD and merged into the Data Processing System. I was not in the function that was moving to Bethesda. However, with my Systems Analyst experience, I interviewed for an opportunity to move to Bethesda. Many of the New Jersey residents did not wish to move to Bethesda, so there was a need for my skill. I was accepted to move with the merger. It was not that far south, but it was a great opportunity to get into the Division that was not going away, as was the case for the Office Products Division. We had visited DC, and the boys were excited that we could live there and see all the museums as often as we wanted to.

By November of 1983, Kathy and I were on a house hunting trip to MD. When we returned home, Lee asked us if we looked in Virginia. He explained that he and his best friend, John Camper, were planning to attend college in Virginia and that if we lived in Virginia it would reduce the cost for college. We were not happy with the choices for the houses we saw in MD. What we could afford were far out with a very long commute.

Kathy and I returned at our own expense and spent two days checking out communities in Virginia. Again, God's plan for us was kept on track by the fact that Lee's friend at Bergen Baptist and he had discussed Virginia colleges. We liked several communities we visited. We found a house and plan we liked. It was the last lot in a small development of two and three acre lots. It was the last lot because it had a shared driveway with the neighbor. I met with the neighbor, Art Rich, and we were friends immediately. We had a lot in common. He and his wife Jewel became great friends for the rest of our days. It would take six months to build, so we would need to rent a house. Our Realtor found a rental in Vienna, the same town for the house we were building. This would ensure that the boys would not have to change schools when we moved to the new house. It was a stretch for us financially. It would mean Kathy would need to work full time. This was okay, because the boys were now old enough to be responsible when they came home from school. The house we bought on Richview Court was the best investment we ever made. We labeled it our "Golden Goose." God for certain had a hand in it.

It was a big task to merge the two systems. We had many planning meetings to develop every detail needed to accomplish the merger without missing a billing cycle. The off and back on switch was to occur over the long Thanksgiving Holiday.

We would not move until December when the boys' Christmas Holiday started. We needed to be settled in the rental house by the time the Christmas break ended for the Virginia schools. Kathy took care of all this process, i.e., closing out the house in New Jersey, getting the boys enrolled in their new schools, getting the rental house ready. As soon as the mover finished unloading in Virginia, we left for our Christmas visit with our parents. Since leaving Mississippi, we never missed our visits back for Christmas and the Fourth of July.

Just before we moved, Steve's friend had a lab puppy he wanted Steve to have. He was half golden retriever, long haired, black lab. We named him Bear. He was the smartest dog we could have ever hoped to own.

169

Chapter 29:

AT HOME IN THE OLD DOMINION

Our move from NJ to Virginia in December, 1983, was our fifth move in twenty years. I promised this was the last move. I would finish my IBM career without another move. Evidently this one time my plan was in sync with God's. Our years in the Washington area were blessed above and beyond our grandest expectations. Our lives were blessed both spiritually and financially. Both our careers exceeded our dreams. Our boy's accomplishments and their growth in their faith in God were the greatest blessings of all. God's timing was in charge of our lives. The attempts I had made to go for a career move to get back closer to our parents had been for naught, because God was saving us for this one last move. When I think of my willingness to be an internal auditor, traveling 80% of the time, I am thankful God closed that door. Trying to get an opportunity in Lexington or Raleigh with the Office Products Division were both met with rejections. Both of these operations went away with the decline and replacement of our IBM Office Products by the Personal Computer. God had a definite reason to bring us to this place at this time.

I don't know how she did it, but with me working extra hours on the team preparing the transfer of the system from OP HQ to

Bethesda, Kathy handled all of the move details which were many, both in leaving New Jersey and getting set up in the rental house in Vienna. More importantly, she had the boy's enrolled and ready for their new schools when Christmas break ended. It was a real concern moving them in the middle of a school year. They were both enjoying their schools and had made friendships at school, and of course they didn't want to leave their close-knit youth group at Bergen Baptist. We were sort of glad that they would no longer be doing treasure hunts in the middle of the night in Hackensack, New Jersey. Kathy was not working at this time, so she devoted full time to the boys and their needs. They were pleased with their schools. Only Steve was upset that his middle school was more like Elementary because they had to stand in line for the cafeteria. In New Jersey they had more freedom and were treated more like high school.

Steve became very engrossed in his studies. He excelled in Math and Computers. I bought our first PC in 1981. Steve became our expert. In high school, he had an exceptional Math teacher. She attended the church we had joined, Columbia Baptist, in Falls Church. She took a special interest in Steve. Upon graduation he received the High School Math Award. He was a National Merit Scholarship Finalist. This meant, as a merit finalist, he received the T J Watson Scholarship awarded to children of IBM Employees. He was accepted into the Engineering School at Duke University. We were very proud of Steve and blessed by his humble attitude that all these honors were no big deal. Steve was happy to study in his room. Maybe he went to a movie on Saturday with a couple of friends from school.

Lee on the other hand was our socialite. He seldom missed a party that he knew about. These were not formal parties. Word was just spread that there was a party at so and so. Then everyone showed up. He had many friends, mostly girls I think. He served as their counselor, giving them advice for resolving whatever problems they brought to him. He and Scott Zimmerman were best friends and went together to all the parties. I believe they kept each other out of trouble. We worried that Lee may be drinking. He said he would hold the same beer and never to our knowledge really drank for getting a high. I cannot believe we allowed him to have two big parties at our house. Once he had a band in our unfinished basement. It was so loud that our neighbor threatened to call the cops, even though I had warned her it would be loud, but we would end it at 11 pm. The kids disappeared in seconds when I told them the cops were on the way. Lee never caused any problems. He handled his having a good time in a very mature manner.

He was also a good student. He was interested in so many things, philosophy, history, social studies, politics and government. He could have conversations with anyone about anything and loved to argue his points. Seemed only natural for him to become a lawyer. His SAT scores were good, and he applied to several colleges. He was accepted at William & Mary. We were very proud of him. William & Mary was small and accepted only a small percentage of the total applicants each year. He excelled in his college studies and early on set his goal for Law School. I believe because of his outstanding record he was accepted in the Law School at William & Mary. His seven years there at the beautiful campus and wonderful town of Williamsburg was about as good as it gets. We enjoyed every visit there, which was often.

The many prayers by our parents for Kathy and me and for Lee and Steve have been answered time and time again. Lee and Steve never caused us any problem of any kind. They had to contend with the drug culture and the results of the 60's sexual revolution. Their faithful attendance to Sunday School and church, involvement in church youth groups and then Inter-Varsity all during their college years enabled them to grow in their faith. That is something I failed to do for many years after I graduated from high school. They and their families continue to faithfully live for Christ in their daily walk.

After we were settled in the rental house in Vienna, we became friends with our neighbors Peter and Ginger Sparber. Peter was a lobbyist for the tobacco industry. He had an office in DC. Later, when Kathy decided to set up her own CPA practice, Sparber & Associates was her major client. Peter also served on the Board of CrossLink International.

DC had so much to offer for our boys. They were interested in the museums and the many historical sites. We spent many Saturday's in downtown DC taking in all these free educational and worthy venues. Our appreciation for our great country grew as we learned more about our history and the sacrifices made by so many. Steve learned all the historical tourist must-sees and served as the tour guide for our friends and kin folk that visited us and wanted to see the DC sites.

About the time our house on Richview Court was completed, Kathy interviewed with a small two partner CPA firm in Fairfax, Virginia. Hoffman and Dykes were two young CPA's that had just started their firm. Their office was a townhouse. Within a couple of years, they had outgrown that space. They moved into a spacious building in Vienna much closer to where we lived. The small firm grew, and in a few years, Kathy was Manager for the small business clients. She had a staff of three people but was still putting in many extra hours. Kathy was so dedicated and thorough in her work that the long hours, especially at tax season, led Kathy to decide to resign and set up her own private practice. She could control how many clients and the amount of time she would be working. Hoffman and Dykes were interested in growing their firm and they kept pushing more and more work onto their employees.

We had both lost our respect for Hoffman and Dyke. They had a client that was in oil speculation. He solicited money for financing of drilling that was assured to become a big oil producer. Hoffman and Dyke claimed they had been very successful investing with this client and made substantial returns when the venture struck oil. Kathy and I were offered an opportunity to invest in a venture in Louisiana. I knew Louisiana was rich in oil reserves, and they assured us it was a safe investment. Initially, only five thousand was required. But, as the drilling progressed, many additional payments were needed to continue the drilling. After fifty thousand, all of our hard-earned savings for college were used up. There was still no oil producing well. We didn't know how many more clients were contributing to the same well. He sent letters describing the excellent potential that was showing as a result of the drilling and then added this much more money was required for continuing to drill. We decided to quit and suffer our loses. From our viewpoint it looked like a scam. We never heard any more about whether the venture was successful. It was an expensive lesson to learn, but we never again speculated with our money to make a fast buck. God always provided for us.

Our house in Vienna turned out to be the golden goose for us and provided all the funds we needed for the boy's college expenses. The DC area benefited greatly from the housing boom. Our equity grew every year. Tax laws allowed us to have a second mortgage for financing any major expenditure. We had Lee entering college in 1986 and Steve in 1988. We used our second mortgage as we needed for any college expenses.

Our Golden Goose

Steve was offered a good scholarship to attend Virginia Tech. After we visited the campus, for whatever reason, Steve decided he would prefer to look elsewhere. He had applied and was accepted at Duke University. He was impressed that Duke's Engineering School was small compared to Virginia Tech's huge engineering presence so he elected to go to Duke.

Since Duke was so expensive, I suggested that he check out the ROTC program. He applied and was accepted into the Air Force ROTC. He decided early on that he did not want to have a four-year hitch in the Air Force after graduation, but he stuck with it through his Junior year. He didn't want to burden us with the extra expense, especially, since he had turned down the Virginia Tech scholarship. The National Merit Scholarship was based on need, so it covered only a small amount of Duke's charges. At the end of his Junior year, Steve dropped out of ROTC. He signed an agreement to repay the scholarship monies in monthly installments for three years. After graduation, Steve landed a great programming job in the DC area, moved in with us and paid the ROTC loan back in one year. Since it was an interest free loan, it was a terrific deal.

Steve was disappointed in the quality of his engineering courses at Duke. The summer after his Sophomore year, he talked to me about transferring to William & Mary and majoring in History. I encouraged him to stay with Engineering since he was blessed with exceptional talents for that career. He would have something to fall back on no matter what work he chose. He decided to stay at Duke and earn an Engineering degree. After he was hired by Sprint and paid the ROTC loan back, he then bought a two-bedroom condo near his work. One of his InterVarsity friends, Jeff, was working in Northern Virginia. He moved in with Steve and paid rent. Steve now had some assistance with the cooking.

Both Lee and Steve maintained contact with their InterVarsity friends living in the Northern Virginia area. During the summers while in college, they would have Bible Study and prayer services at our house. It was a wonderful blessing to witness them put their faith into action in fellowship with fellow Christians. We encouraged and were happy to accommodate them. We were blessed to see them continue to worship during their summer break.

Lee was successful in all of his studies at W&M. He knew early on that he wanted to be a lawyer. His courses were geared to that end result. He had a wonderful circle of friends in InterVarsity, and he continued to counsel those that brought their problems to his attentive ears. Some of the guys have remained friends and they try to get together at least once each year. Marty, the InterVarsity Pastor, also remained a close friend of the guys. Lee was extremely happy that he was accepted by the W&M Law School. We purchased a townhouse near the Law School. Lee kept enough students renting that it paid the monthly mortgage. His only expense was his tuition. He gained recognition in Law School with his outstanding performance in Moot Court, traveling one year to New York for a competition.

Both Lee and Steve were blessed to have good paying summer jobs. They saved all of their earnings since they were staying with us. They used their savings for their spending money at school. Even though both had a car at school, we had to provide very little spending money for them.

During Lee's last year in Law School, he met Kris Looney. They were both in InterVarsity. After graduating from Duke, she was at W&M for their Special Education Master's program. Lee was in love instantly. Kris needed some convincing. Lee was not about to give up. In the end, he was successful. He arranged for a very special place to actually propose to Kris. He asked the caretaker for the Wren building to open it on this specific night so he could propose to Kris in this very special building on campus. Jefferson had actually attended classes in the Wren building. Lee had spent the weekend before at home with us. We shopped with him for the rings. He had researched all the criteria for judging a high quality diamond. He has always shown that same quality level in the way of expressing his love for Kris throughout their marriage. They planned to be married on May 8, 1993, as soon as they graduated.

Happy, Soon to Married Graduates

Kris planned every detail of the most beautiful wedding that can be imagined. The day was beautiful, the Spring flowers were all in bloom and the church was decorated beautifully. It was as if God had smiled down on their love for each other. We were blessed beyond words seeing their happiness and knowing their vows were real, not only before the huge attendance, but more importantly before God. Many of our family from Mississippi came for the wedding. Mother had passed away in 1990. Kris's Mother's parents had also passed away, so they were acknowledged and honored in the service. My Dad made it fine through the wedding ceremony, but when they walked him to the back at the end of the service, Dad hugged me and said he wished Mother could have been there. Then he broke down and cried. We all cried, for it was a time of joy and our hearts were full. When our sons got married, I feel that the joy I experienced was as close to the joy we will experience in heaven as we can have here on earth.

A Beautiful, Beautiful Wedding

They made their home in Charlottesville. Lee had a one-year internship with Judge Criggler.

Kris would teach at Forest Lakes Elementary. They bought their first house in Forest Lakes.

Lee was hired by an old, prestigious law firm, Trembley and Smith. He trained under one of the most successful medical malpractice attorneys in Virginia. Lee has maintained that specialty and has been very successful. For a few years he had his own firm. He had so much business he just could not handle all that goes with maintaining a one lawyer firm. Kris handled all the administrative work that she could. When offered the opportunity, he merged his clients into a very old and reputable firm. He has been very successful with this firm.

When our granddaughter, Annalise, was born in September, 1999, we drove to Martha Jefferson Hospital to welcome our very first grandchild. We were thankful she was a healthy beautiful baby. Then in May 2001, we welcomed our grandson Daniel. When Daniel was less than a year old, it was evident his motor skills were not developing normally. He was having mild seizures. The doctor believed he had MS. After testing at Johns Hopkins, it was determined that he had a very rare genetic disease, Glut One Protein Deficiency Syndrome.

Since that time, Kris has been the wonderful and dedicated caretaker for Daniel. He has a specific diet that requires weighing the contents of every meal. Absolutely no carbohydrates or sugars. She tutors him in all subjects. The sacrifice she has made and is making has made a huge difference in Daniel's life. Daniel is outgoing, positive, self-confident and is loved by everyone that knows him. He has made great strides improving his motor skills. He can beat his Dad at basketball. Kris should have many gold medals for the unbelievable dedication to the efforts she has made on behalf of Daniel. Her Master's in Special Education has been put to the test, but not how she would have preferred. Daniel is now a Senior at Albemarle High School. Annalise finished at Albemarle with special honors and is now a Junior at James Madison University. She is a leader in InterVarsity and a Resident Aid. She is loving college life. She was a camp counselor at a Christian camp in Texas last summer. She plans a trip to Ireland in the summer of 2019. We have been very blessed to live near Lee, Kris, Annalise and Daniel. We have enjoyed many, many celebrations for birthdays, holidays and school activities the way we did with our parents when Lee and Steve were growing up.

Lee and Kris have honored us in so many ways, but most importantly, by their Christian witness. They are both active in their church, Lee serving as an Elder and Kris teaches a Bible Study. In 2017, Lee was elected President of the Virginia Trial Lawyers Association. In 2019 he received the Southern Trial Lawyers Lighthouse Award. They have raised Annalise and Daniel to believe in and live their lives in fellowship with their Savior and fellow Christians. Hallelujah and Amen!

Upon graduation from Duke, Steve landed a temporary job with IBM. We rode to work together until he got a permanent job with Sprint. Lee's friend, Scott Zimmerman, was working for Sprint and told Steve they were hiring. Sprint and Alcatel, the French Telephone Company, formed a joint venture. Steve became part of the Alcatel organization. He had the opportunity to travel to Paris and work with the engineers at Alcatel. He was impressed with their two-hour lunches that included wine with their meal. While on duty in France, Steve toured Paris and the French countryside, including Normandy. There were many very old historic churches. One weekend he traveled to London on the express train from Paris that goes under the English Channel.

Steve attended Reston Bible Church, but maintained friend-ship with former Bible study friends from Columbia Baptist. He went with a group on several mission trips to El Salvador. They did manual labor at an orphanage. Steve felt God was calling him to become a missionary in Central America. God not only called him, but also provided a financial solution for him to attend Seminary. Sprint and Alcatel dissolved their joint venture. Steve was paid a large severance amount, sufficient for attending Seminary if he commuted to Capital Bible Seminary in Maryland. He moved back in with us, and in three years graduated as the Valedictorian of his class. It was a great honor for us to have him obtain his Master of Divinity degree, but was unsettling not knowing what was in Steve's future as a missionary. I encouraged him to get associated with the Southern Baptist Mission Board. They were a large organization that would provide the support and benefits he would need for a career as a missionary. Instead he and classmate friend, Tom Gill, established a house church in Southern Maryland near where Tom lived.

Steve Graduates Valedictorian from Capital Bible Seminary

Shortly thereafter, Steve learned of a Christian organization from Texas, World Gospel Outreach (WGO), that had a mission house in Honduras that provided support for short term medical mission groups that came to Honduras from churches in the US. The mission house provided food and lodging for these groups and laid the groundwork for where the medical aid was most needed. WGO also operated a ranch in the mountains fifteen miles from

Tegucigalpa. The ranch was a group of houses for children assigned by the state due to their situation at their home. Each home had house parents and six to eight children that they were responsible for raising in a Christian and loving environment. Steve interviewed and was accepted to work for WGO. He had to raise his own funds for his living expenses and was paid no salary. This seemed to be what Steve preferred, a real sacrifice for his Lord and Savior.

Steve became the house parent for seven boys ages seven to sixteen. He had a full time and a part time Honduran lady that cooked and cleaned and helped discipline the boys. Steve was responsible for their studies, social skills and becoming knowledgeable of the Bible. And most importantly, how to live a life centered on Jesus Christ. Steve also taught at the Ranch school.

Kathy and I were blessed that we were able to visit Steve and the boys at the Ranch several times for a stay of one week each trip. We stayed in Steve's room and lived with Steve and the boys. We saw firsthand the difficult job that Steve had. The boys were very kind and nice to us and we loved each of them. They did not always get along with each other, just like all children. Steve's goal was for all of them to graduate from High School. They had to leave the Ranch and live on their own after graduation. Three were going to work toward getting a college degree. Some were able to find jobs. Some had difficulties. It is a very hard life in Honduras for the poor. At least the boys have a high school education that will help them compete for work. By 2009, after five years serving in Honduras, Steve decided to return to the US and work in the Maryland church and do some tutoring to earn some income.

Both Lee and Steve have brought only honor and thanksgiving to us. We have been blessed by them beyond any measure of our deserving. I give Kathy all the credit for their early childhood development. Our prayers and the prayers of our parents were answered more boldly by our Father in Heaven than by the meager requests that we made. Both boys and their families are honoring us by honoring God with their work for their loving Savior's kingdom on this earth. This is the utmost joy that can be expected of Kathy and myself here on this earth. This beautiful thing called church!

The many successes of my family after we moved to Virginia also included my IBM career. Within two months of the successful move and merger of the OP System into the DP System, I was asked to manage a purchase team in the DP Administration Division. This was a big advance for me. The industry was changing so rapidly, and computer power was getting smaller and smaller. IBM realized that the Big Iron we were leasing to customers would soon have no market value. So IBM had a huge bargain sale for the installed lease inventory. I had a great team and enjoyed a nice window office in a new building in Rockville, Maryland. Nearly all my team were women, much younger than me, so I was treated like their Dad. I was always fair in managing, and they respected my decisions. After three years, the purchase activity was closed down.

I was asked to join a team assigned to develop Quality Processes for the Administrative Functions. Quality Process was a new concept that was being implemented in many large companies like IBM. It had started in Manufacturing. I was chosen for this assignment because of my experience in the Branch Office and as a System Analyst in Headquarters. This project lasted two years.

There was an opening for Manager of the Internal Administration and Controls department in the Headquarters Services Division. This department reported to the Headquarters Services Division in Atlanta. The Manager there was Ed Miller. He had previously been an Area Manager in Office Products Division. He and my brother Carey were Area Managers together and were good friends. When he found out I was Carey's brother, he interviewed me and hired me on the spot. I worked for Ed many years and we became good friends.

I was now assigned to the Headquarters Services Division of IBM, which turned out to be the best move that could have ever happened to me. When we moved from New Jersey in December 1983, I had already completed over twenty years of service. This meant in ten years I would be eligible for retirement with thirty years of service. Not that I planned to retire at age fifty four. By 1990, IBM began to offer incentive programs for employees to retire early. This was a way to avoid lay-offs, which was a sacred policy of which IBM was very proud. IBM needed to reduce their expenses.

The Quality Process Work had resulted in the Company's goal of maintaining only the processes that were their core business. This meant eliminating things like Administrative Services, Personnel and Payroll and many other functions that had nothing to do with Manufacturing, Servicing, Programming and Selling Computers, which were the core businesses for IBM. In 1992, IBM began to contract out these functions that were not part of their core business. The entire Headquarters Services Division was contracted out to Tascor, a company set up by IBM and a Personnel Services Company in Atlanta. I would have the same job, at the same salary as Manager of the Internal Administration and Controls. I was also given one year's salary plus medical benefits as severance payment. One year later, at the completion of 30 years of service, I would start drawing my retirement pay. This was a financial windfall. God's plan had put me in the right place at the right time. I worked for Tascor seven years.

At the age of sixty one, I resigned. The work became more and more stressful. My assignment was managing a contract at the Manassas, Virginia plant. This contract employed thirty people performing the administrative services in the plant. There was constant personnel turnover, for these were minimum paying jobs that required only a high school education. This work was too much for an old man. Kathy and I had been saving the maximum allowed for our 401K accounts. Unless there was a major financial meltdown, we had sufficient retirement salaries and savings for a comfortable retirement.

As the amazingly good fortune was occurring in my IBM and Tascor career, Kathy had even more unbelievable events happening in her career. And more importantly, these were opportunities for her to be involved in the things of God's Kingdom right here on earth. She was employed by Prison Fellowship International, a Christian organization dedicated to helping prisoners learn about and accept Christ as their Savior. She was also an original Board Member of CrossLink, a Christian charity dedicated to providing medical supplies and non-prescription medicines to the poor in the United States and Third World countries.

When Kathy left Hoffman and Dykes, she set up her solo CPA practice in our home. She had four major clients and some smaller clients, all obtained by word of mouth by friends and former clients from Hoffman and Dykes. These were some wonderful years in Kathy's career. She was her own boss, could work at her own pace, and most of all enjoyed the friendships she had with her clients. They appreciated her honest dealings and attention to detail. None of her clients were ever called in for audit by the IRS. She was very proud of that accomplishment. Her workload increased and many hours were required, especially at tax time. She just did not have the energy for all the work. During this time, I was also working full time so was not much help at home for her. I also think that about this time her thyroid ceased to perform adequately. About three years later it completely stopped working, and she practically collapsed when we were on a weekend trip to North Carolina looking at possible retirement towns. When she was examined the next Monday morning, Doctor Beyer could not believe she was able to walk. Her thyroid was completely dead. We had no way of knowing how long the decline in its function had gone on. She had never explained her symptoms to her doctor. She was always positive and never complained to him of being tired and exhausted.

We were very thankful to learn there is a prescription pill that can replace the thyroid function. It took some time to get her thyroid functioning properly. The high dose caused her to be hyper and the low dose caused her to be drowsy. The correct balance was alternating the daily dose. There are some studies that connect thyroid issues with Alzheimer's.

At this time, her biggest and best paying client, Sparber and Associates, had grown and needed to hire a larger CPA firm to handle all of their work, including payroll. Even though he offered to have Kathy set up an office in DC to handle just his work, she decided it was just too much to attempt. Had she been younger and not had thyroid issues it would have been doable. But God had much better work lined up for Kathy. After leaving the Sparber account, she decided she would gradually have the rest of her clients find another CPA to handle their work. Over a period of a year she gradually had no more clients.

She continued to do free tax returns for family members and for Mandy, the lady that cleaned our house. Mandy kept very poor records for her cleaning service. Kathy had to construct her tax return from the various receipts and bank statements that she provided. She was from El Salvador and had two small boys. I felt sorry for her. I was led to start a 529 College fund for her two boys. I contributed $100 a month for each of them for this fund. One attended college and used both funds. He graduated from James Mason University and is employed by Fairfax County. The other son did not go to college. Instead he got married and is a manager for an automobile service company. He has two children.

Mandy's cleaning service was primarily in the affluent area of Vienna. She had several employees she would drop off and then come back around and make sure they were doing a good job. She was a devout Catholic. Her church provided English classes. She was soon fluent in English. She eventually was hired by Costco to work in the fast food shop at the front of the store. After a few years, because she was a very reliable employee, she was promoted to run a checkout register, which she still does today. When Kathy and I retired to Ruckersville, she came down to visit us and see our new home. She mentioned that she would come down once a month and continue to provide her cleaning service for us. She still comes once a month on her day off and cleans our house. She has cleaned our house now for over 33 years and is a dear friend.

While Kathy was not working, we would visit Lee at William and Mary and Steve at Duke. On a holiday weekend we would visit towns in North Carolina thinking we may like to retire to North Carolina. After a few months off and with her thyroid now working, Kathy mentioned she was thinking she might want to find a part time job. She had worked all of her life, even summers in high school. She was not about to sit at home and knit.

Chapter 30:

THE PRISON MINISTRY

><|<

Soon after a sabbatical of a few months, Kathy decided she needed to find a part time job. At that time there was a recession resulting in high unemployment. Jobs were in short supply. In an effort to help the membership that might be in need of work, Columbia Baptist Church compiled a binder that contained the openings for jobs provided by various members of the church. I did not even know about the binder. I was early one evening for a deacons meeting and noticed the binder on a table in the hallway. I picked it up and quickly thumbed through it while waiting for my meeting to start. Then this one single page caught my eye. A part time accountant was needed by Prison Fellowship International(PFI). I had read that Chuck Colson, Nixon's hatchet man, had founded a prison ministry after he was released from prison. I jotted down the contact information, and when I got home, I casually mentioned the opening to Kathy and suggested she call and request an interview. We both agreed it would be a blessing to work for a Christian charitable organization. I told her if she was the right person for the job it would be God's will for her to get the job. I felt God had led me to this binder since Kathy was interested in a part time job. Kathy called and gave the contact person, Greg

Strong, information about her qualifications and experience. Greg agreed for her to come in for an interview. We became excited. We prayed for God's will, that if she got the job, we would know it was His will. If she did not get the job, we would know it was not His will. Greg was the office manager. He was very impressed with Kathy in the interview, not only her qualifications and experience but also her Christian background. He emphasized that before a person was hired by Prison Fellowship Ministries (PFM), they were required to sign a statement of Christian beliefs and promised to live in accordance with those beliefs. This was not a problem for Kathy. Greg then scheduled for her to interview with the President of Prison Fellowship International, Ron Nichol. The only issue he had was that the job did not require a CPA, and since they were a charity, the pay was much lower than equivalent work in the commercial world. This was fine with Kathy. She wanted the job because it would be rewarding to work for a worthy Christian cause. Within days, she was called to report to work at their office located only ten minutes from our home. A ten-minute commute in the DC area was a very welcome benefit.

The accounting project that needed Kathy's expertise was to set up the accounting process for PFI that was currently being done by PFM, the domestic arm of the ministry. The accounting needed to be separate to provide an accurate accounting picture for the two separate ministries. Kathy had experience in setting up accounting systems and choosing software. She was the right person at the right place at the right time. Where had we heard that before? We still did not have any idea what God had in store for us, especially for Kathy. After the initial system work was finished, she now had to get the accounting work in all the countries where PFI had established offices tied into the new accounting system. This was a much more difficult task. Usually there was only a single person in each office that handled all the expenses and income for the Director for the country. These two people were the only paid employees. The remaining workers for teaching and training in the prisons were all volunteers.

After a year, it was evident that Kathy was needed full time. The office in the US was growing and additional offices were being added as additional countries joined the ministry. Soon after she started working full time, an assistant was hired for her. Kathy worked for PFI for nine years.

It was her greatest accomplishment. She was doing God's work. That is a good feeling. I even got to taste a little of that feeling later on as a result of Kathy's next career move.

Kathy had an important role in promoting God's Kingdom here on earth. Prior to our knowledge of the work of PFM, our attitude about prisoners was lock them up and throw away the key. We began to realize that their lives needed to be changed by the saving grace of Jesus Christ. Otherwise, when they were released, there was a very high percent that would get back into crime and be caught and returned. Our wrongful attitude was changed. The treatment and conditions for prisoners in some of the foreign countries was horrible. The US prisons were like plush hotels compared to some in third world countries. PFI worked with government officials in these countries to address the many problems that needed to be fixed. The foreign officials were receptive to all the work PFI was doing to get improvements. They also allowed more freedom to teach the Bible and witness to prisoners than was allowed in the US, because in the US there were concerns of separation of church and state. There were programs allowed in the US if they were designed to ensure that all prisoners attending Bible studies and prayer services were volunteering to do so. PFI and PFM both worked diligently to create unique programs and opportunities for the many Christian volunteers to come into the prisons and share the good news of the saving power of Jesus Christ.

At some point, Kathy earned the title of Controller for PFI. She had the expertise to establish accounting checks and balances and the personality to win over any objections by management to implement proper accounting controls. She had the opportunity to travel to several countries to train and audit the accounting operations for the PFI office in that country. Everyone Kathy dealt with loved her. There was always at least one person in the office that could speak English. Over time Kathy traveled to Switzerland, Peru, Zimbabwe, Bulgaria and Canada.

I had the opportunity to join her for a short visit in some of the countries at the completion of her work. We saw Switzerland, Peru and Canada together. In Switzerland, we did a train tour through the Alps. The snowy mountain scenery was breath taking, very beautiful just like the pictures. We were changing trains in a major train station with trains for several different cities. We got on the wrong train. I was watching the names of the towns where the train stopped and with my map determined we were headed in the wrong direction. We got off and had to wait an hour before the next train we needed. We were starved so we walked a block to this small deserted cafe and ordered what we thought was a hamburger. But it was a horse burger. We ate only half of it. The waitress could not speak English. We took the train to the Airport when we were leaving for home. We got off on the wrong stop. The town name was almost the same as the town name where we were to get off. The station was completely deserted, not a person in sight. As we were removing our luggage from the train, a lady came flying from behind the building waving her arms indicating for us to get back on the train. They held the train long enough for us to get our luggage and ourselves back on the train. We only saw the woman for a few seconds, but I have maintained that she looked exactly like my Aunt Madge that had passed away several years previously. I believe God sent an angel to guide us dummies.

In Peru we visited Machu Picchu and witnessed the amazing structures built by the Incas. We were stranded overnight in Cuzco because the only plane out had flat tires. We could not speak a word of Spanish, so Kathy called the person that worked in the PFI office in Peru and she got us a room in the nicest hotel in Cuzco. It was sad to see the poor people in Peru. At every turn, the ladies were selling their beautiful handmade wares of clothing, dishes and art. On the bus trip on the narrow winding road up the mountain to Machu Picchu, children ran alongside the slow-moving bus begging for US dollars. Seeing the poverty in Peru caused me to realize how blessed we are to live in the United States.

Kathy's years with PFI were remarkable times for both of us. I know God had guided my career with many opportunities and closed some doors that were my own plans. In Kathy's case, the circumstances were such that it was a living testimony that God is involved in our daily lives and has direct control of, not only world events, but every aspect of our lives if we are living in His will. The fact that I happened to look at the jobs available binder at Columbia Baptist and saw the opening for a part time accountant at PFI, and the fact that for the first time in Kathy's career she was not employed but thinking about looking for a part time job, and then the fact that she was the best qualified applicant for the project. All of this could not possibly have been just coincidences. The prayers by PFI were answered by having a candidate that fit their project exactly and was a devoted Christian that would have no problem signing their Statement of Faith requirement.

Kathy's very successful nine years at PFI resulted in her moving to PFM as Controller. When the position came open, some on the accounting staff at PFM encouraged her to apply for the job. Based on Kathy's reputation at PFI, they believed she would be a good person to manage their department. Kathy applied for the position. There was always competition between managers for PFI and PFM. In this case, PFI accused PFM of recruiting Kathy. Chuck Colson had to approve the move anyway, so he approved because Kathy had earned the promotion.

The controller position for PFM was no cake walk. She managed six experienced staff and maintained accounting control and audit of income and expenses exceeding fifty million dollars. For certain, this was the most responsible job she had ever held. The year was 2000, the year I had resigned from Tascor. I encouraged Kathy to take the big job, promising that since I would be home, I would be supportive and do all the cooking, cleaning and grocery shopping so she could be fully devoted to her new responsibility.

Her success as Controller for PFM brought not only financial benefits but the title of Vice-President Controller. Our Pastor at Columbia Baptist, Neal Jones, was a board member for PFM. He nominated Kathy for Vice-President and the board unanimously approved. Kathy's hard work, perseverance and intelligence enabled her to become a CPA. Now this remarkable accomplishment had resulted in the most successful career that either of us could have ever imagined in 1977 when we discussed whether or not she should sit for the CPA exam. I was very, very proud for Kathy. You would think I would have been just a little jealous that she had surpassed me in both compensation and title. However, my joy for her was about more than money and title. She was the joy of my life. She had brought me true happiness from that first day we met after choir practice at East Central Community College. She had accomplished the most important role in God's plan for her, and that is being a loving mother and wife, and raising two children to be God loving Christians. I know she had the many, many prayers of our parents and God's guidance along the way. Kathy stayed strong in her faith and always tried to stay in God's will in her daily life.

Just as Kathy was thinking of retirement and start drawing her Social Security check, God had one more blessing for us both to share as a result of our being associated with Prison Fellowship Ministries. PF had outgrown their office facilities in Reston, VA only ten minutes from where we lived. Kathy would now have to commute ten miles to the new PFM campus In Leesburg, VA. The beautiful new office building would provide room for growth for both PFM and PFI. Sale of the property in Reston was enough to pay for the new facility.

In addition to the office facilities, a new ten room Guest House was built a few steps away from the new office. The Guest House provided rooms for PF personnel and volunteers attending training classes held at the new office. Each room had a private bath. A one-bedroom apartment on the first floor was provided for Chuck and Patty when they were in town for board meetings and PF business in the Washington area. A two-bedroom apartment on the second floor was provided for the yet to be named Guest House host. Kathy casually mentioned that they were looking for a host couple to live in the Guest House. For some reason my thought was to check into the details and see if we qualified for the job. In the back of my mind I was thinking it would save Kathy the long commute if we lived next door to the office. By this time the job was getting harder and harder for Kathy. She was working later and later and even on Saturdays. It could be that Alzheimer's changes were already beginning to affect her performance.

Kathy came home all excited with details of the requirements of the Host's job. Responsible for security of the Guest House 24/7. Responsible for preparing breakfast for the guests. Responsible for grocery shopping for the breakfast foods. Responsible for providing a friendly welcome and give any assistance the guest needed to make their stay comfortable and enjoyable. We did not supervise the cleaning service, but we were to check the rooms and baths for proper cleaning to ensure they were ready for occupancy and report any concerns to the Facilities Manager. Since Kathy would be working during the day, most of the duties would be my responsibility. Tim Robinson interviewed us, and we were accepted. Since Kathy had already begun thinking about retirement, we requested that the assignment be for only two years with the option to extend if our retirement plans changed. Things had to move fast. The Guest House was scheduled to be completed February 1, 2005. Our two-bedroom apartment was furnished, so all we needed to move were clothing, sheets, bath towels and kitchen utensils. A TV was even furnished. So, moving was no problem. I could travel back to Vienna during the day and get anything we needed from our house.

Even though we moved in on February 1st, 2005, there were no guests scheduled the first month. There were some final inspections and insurance considerations that were being finalized. I felt that I would have no problem preparing breakfast. I had helped Kathy do our breakfast on Sundays after church for a group of hungry guys. They loved Kathy's biscuits, my crisp fried bacon and scrambled eggs. The Guest House breakfast would be fruits, cereals, bagels, toast, pastries, bacon, eggs cooked to order, coffee and juices. The number of guests scheduled was always provided, in order for me to keep the grocery pantry and refrigerator stocked with sufficient supplies. I received many compliments for my breakfasts.

Kathy and I both made many friends from all over the world as they came through the Guest House. She already knew and was known by many of the PFI guests that came in for meetings, now that PFI was in the same office building. The guests were overly complimentary of our Southern hospitality. We could have stayed for years doing this enjoyable service for this very worthy and needed Christian ministry and for the wonderful Christian workers and volunteers. However, I was almost sixty-eight and Kathy was becoming overwhelmed at work. We had saved for retirement and decided we needed to retire soon in order to be able to enjoy retirement and travel some.

Kathy gave her resignation letter to retire from PFM effective February 1, 2006. This date would coincide with our two-year commitment to serve the Guest House. We would have all of 2006 to serve together at the Guest House and work on our retirement plan. We would need to be ready to move on February 1, 2007.

We had settled on Charlottesville, VA since our son Lee and his family were settled there and it was a great small city with beautiful mountain scenery. We purchased in a new development for fifty five and older in Ruckersville, VA, thirteen miles north of Charlottesville. The completion of construction of our new home would coincide with the planned retirement date. We had sold our home in Vienna at the end of 2005, anticipating that we would move directly from the Guest house to our retirement. We placed our furniture in storage. We vested the proceeds from the sale of our home in CD's.

Hovnanian had an identical development in Northern Virginia and a Center that displayed all the many options we could choose from for our new home. It was difficult to decide on the many choices we had. Kathy was already getting to a point that decisions were very difficult for her. It seemed most of the decisions were up to me. One extra option that I purchased special for Kathy was a speaker system for every room. Kathy loved music and this was a special surprise for her. It has been a great blessing to her as music is one thing she can still enjoy. My not knowing at this time how important the music would be, again, God was taking care of even the little things in our lives.

This great new housing development turned out to be not so great. Just as the beautiful, extravagant club house designed to accommodate five hundred families was completed came the horrific housing market crash of 2008. The national builder, Hovnanian, stopped the development and never finished many of the promised amenities. And even worse, now only one hundred twenty families would be responsible for operating and maintaining the massive club house. For months the residents met with attorneys and government representatives in an effort to hold Hovnanian accountable for the circumstances that we were facing. We obtained a one time financial payment compensating for the promised amenities that were never completed. These monies were not sufficient to cover all the exposure we now live with for long term maintenance of the club house. This turn of events caused by the financial crisis from the housing market crash impacted our home values. We are very thankful that we sold our home in Northern Virginia before the housing market crash, and our investment in that house was the best investment we ever made. It was very sad to sell the wonderful home we loved for twenty-one years. It had blessed us in so many ways. Our Columbia Baptist church family had become such an important and meaningful part of our lives, this move was really, really difficult. Having moved so many times before, I believe we had faith and confidence that God would continue to guide this next phase of our lives.

With Kathy not working, she shared the duties as host for the Guest House with me. We were also busy with choosing the options for the house and making quick trips to Ruckersville to check on the building progress for our house. One day I received a call from Tim Robinson, the Vice President that had hired us. He asked if I could take the PF Station wagon and pick up Chuck and Patty at the Airport. Of course I would be glad to do it. We had already become friends with them, for they would stay in their apartment on the first floor when they were in town for meetings. They were very friendly and easy to talk to. They never asked us to do anything for them. They did their own meals and Patty did her grocery shopping, even though I asked if I could shop for her. They declined the time I asked if I could do breakfast for them. I would be nervous picking them up because I didn't want to have them waiting. Thankful for cell phones, Chuck and I had a system that worked well. They almost always flew into Reagan National which had a car waiting area without having to go into the short-term parking.

I would park there well before arrival time. Chuck would call me as soon as the plane landed and he was allowed to use his phone. I was always waiting when they stepped out of the terminal. They did not have checked luggage for they had clothes at the apartment.

I used our Buick to pick them up because I was more comfortable driving it. The old Ford station wagon known as "The Chuck Wagon" was not a comfortable ride, and I was afraid it might break down. They seemed to appreciate me using my car. Chuck suggested for me to request mileage expense and I let him know that this was an honor for me to get to do this job. Once we were busy talking, and I almost moved out of my lane but saw the car in the lane beside me just in time to pull back. It was on Patty's side, and she gave a slight jump. Chuck always rode up front, and Patty rode in the back. Kathy sometimes came along and rode in the back with Patty. Once I had to take Chuck downtown to DC to catch a train. It was stormy and raining. Chuck did not like to fly in bad weather. I was not quite sure how to get to the train station. He was talking on the phone and giving me directions with his hand signals. I told him he did a great job getting me to the train on time.

The most exposure to the public that I had as driver for Chuck and Patty was on the Sundays they rode with us to church. At some point we learned that they were members of Columbia Baptist. One weekend when they were in town staying at their apartment in the Guest House, I asked them if they would like to ride to church with us. They agreed. Parking was scarce at Columbia. I would drop them off at the steps then search for a parking spot. They would save me a seat. After church, they waited at the front steps while I brought the car around to pick them up. There was usually a short wait, for folks were always shaking hands and speaking to Chuck and Patty. I felt honored to be the driver for them.

As the driver for Chuck and Patty, one particular destination gave us the opportunity of a lifetime. We drove Chuck and Patty to the East Wing of the White House for a dinner with President and Mrs. George Bush. Bush was having Mr. and Mrs. Gerson for dinner on the occasion of Mr. Gerson's leaving his position as speech writer for the President. Chuck had recommended Gerson for the job. Chuck and George Bush had become good friends when George was Governor of Texas. He authorized a special program for Prison Fellowship to conduct in the Texas prisons. The program had greatly reduced recidivism for the prisoners released. Before we could drive our car onto the grounds of the White House, first our Social Security number, Driver's License and auto license were provided to the FBI for checking all our records for unlawful activity. This was done about a week before the date of the dinner. Then as we entered the grounds, the hood and trunk were opened, and a bomb sniffing dog was led around our car. Then we moved to a metal gate that opened automatically, and finally we were directed by a security officer to a parking spot near the entrance to the White House. Chuck said he would call my cell phone about thirty minutes before it was time for them to leave. He handed me a hundred dollar bill and told us to have a nice dinner. Of course I tried to refuse it, but he insisted. He was very thoughtful and generous.

Chuck and Patty honored us with a lunch when we retired as host for the Colson Family Guest House

When we retired as Host for the Guest House, Chuck and Patty gave a lunch at the Guest House for Kathy and me and the entire Accounting Department. He and Patty gave us a four hundred dollar check and asked that we buy something for our new house. We bought the clutch in our foyer where we display many of our Prison Fellowship and Chuck Colson keepsakes, such as an autographed copy of "Born Again." We were both shocked and saddened when Chuck suddenly collapsed while speaking at a meeting at the hotel near the office in 2012. He passed away a short time later as a result of a brain hemorrhage.

It was a great honor to be invited and attend the celebration of life service for Chuck at the National Cathedral. Knowing Chuck and the change that Christ made in his life after he was "born again" was not only a wonderful blessing to our lives but served as confirmation of our faith and trust in God as our Savior. His was a powerful witness to the prisoners and everyone that met him. He was a living example that God can change a self-centered hatchet man into a humble servant, unselfishly and faithfully serving others.

Chapter 31:

CROSSLINK INTERNATIONAL

➤|⬅

When we moved from New Jersey to Vienna, VA, God led us to join Columbia Baptist Church in Falls Church. We visited Vienna Baptist. It was not your typical Southern Baptist. No one spoke to us. The service and pastor were not impressive. We also visited a church in Tyson's Corner. They had sold their property to the ever expanding shopping district and were building a new facility. We had just been in a building program in New Jersey and didn't wish to join another one at this time. In fact, we were still paying our monthly pledge to fulfill our commitment for the new facility for Bergen Baptist.

I don't know how or from whom we learned about Columbia Baptist. It was fifteen miles from our house. We didn't know anyone there. On our first visit, we were welcomed at the front and asked to provide our information on a visitor card and put it in the offering plate. We were impressed with the beautiful singing by the choir and by the congregation. The Pastor, Neal Jones, was about our age and delivered a very good sermon. Evidently he was well liked, for he had been there fifteen years. We learned he was originally from Texas. Soon we were attending a couples' Sunday

School class. The boys Sunday School teacher was Mrs. Joe Gibbs. We learned that Joe taught a Men's class during off season. Our class had a number of professionals, one doctor, one dentist, one lawyer, two CPA's, several teachers and Denton Lotz, the President of the Baptist World Alliance. He was married to a sister of Billy Graham. God had put all these professionals together, for he had a great plan for this Sunday School class.

At this time, the Soviet Union was in the process of a peaceful change from Communism to a form of Capitalism. This had opened the door for much more bold witness and church attendance. Religions that were practically banned were now free to operate in the open. Columbia Baptist formed a sister relationship with the Moscow Baptist Church, and some of our members went there for a visit. Then some of their members came to visit Columbia. The Columbia choir planned a trip to Moscow Baptist. The wife of Dr. Barry Beyer, the doctor in our class, was a very talented flute player and was going with the choir group to Moscow. Dr. Beyer went along to provide medical assistance. On the visit, he discovered that the Moscow Baptist had been given a run-down hospital that was in need of every kind of hospital supplies and non-prescription medications. He said they were literally washing gauze to be reused. He saw this great need and realized that the hospitals back in the US often threw away many usable supplies because they received a newer version, or the date expired on the supply. When he returned from the trip, he set about contacting hospitals in the Northern VA area and had them send supplies to Columbia Baptist that they were about to discard. The small storage room at church was soon full.

This is how the charity, CrossLink International, was born. CrossLink soon was using a section in a warehouse owned by one of the church members. Volunteers from church would work at night to sort, label, store and enter the items into an inventory control data base. Application for 501(c)(3) status was submitted and approved. A board was established. Kathy was one of the original members of the board and was Secretary of the Board for many years. She also developed the Operations Guide for Personnel and Accounting. The Board and workers were all volunteers, primarily from Columbia. Columbia provided the original seed money to get CrossLink started and paid the salary for the first director. Carey, my brother, became a loyal supporter of CrossLink and also served on the Board for several years. He traveled from North Carolina to the monthly board meetings. He would bring a load of medical supplies he was able to collect in the Raleigh area.

CrossLink International became a huge success. They rented a large warehouse to handle all the donations of medical supplies and non-prescription medicines. Staff was hired. Many volunteers worked nights checking the donations and discarding those that were not acceptable. The inventory system was maintained. The cargo shipments for overseas required special pallets and shrink-wrap. We worked many evenings readying the shipments. Prayers were said for safe delivery of the shipment after we finished getting them loaded onto the truck that was taking them to the dock.

A board member from a Baptist Church in Memphis suggested that a satellite location for CrossLink be established in Memphis. The board authorized the additional site. The operation was on a smaller scale. They prepared the supplies and medicines in small carry on packages for the Christian volunteers going on mission trips to needy countries. This was very well received, and CrossLink-Memphis thrived by providing this much needed support for the many mission trips to third world countries by the Christian churches in the US.

Each year the major fund-raising event for CrossLink International was the Band Aid Ball. This was an extravagant celebration banquet to honor the financial supporters and the many volunteers that made CrossLink possible. This fundraiser helped sustain the operation for many years. Thousands of shipments of needed medical supplies and medicines were sent to many needy hospitals around the world and free clinics in the US. Starting in

2008, CrossLink contributions steadily declined due to the poor economy brought on by the financial crisis and unemployment. CrossLink had the fixed cost for the large warehouse and office space. Even after reduction in paid staff it was evident to the Board that CrossLink International operations could not be maintained. A huge inventory of medical supplies and medicines needed to be made available to another charity that could utilize the inventory. A secular charity in Pittsburgh, PA was willing to merge with CrossLink and absorb the inventory and warehouse cost and some of the support personnel in Falls Church. This was an answer to prayer. The inventory would be saved and be of use without any disruption of service to the many hospitals expecting shipments.

Some of us did not continue to support the new charity because this charity did not provide their services and free medical supplies in the name and for Jesus Christ. CrossLink had always emphasized that the donations were to go to Christian organizations and be used as a witness for Christ. However, many of us continue to support CrossLink Memphis because they continue to maintain that Christian witness by supplying the Christian missions. Many of the original CrossLink family continue their support of CrossLink Memphis. God continues to bless them, and we are thankful the Memphis location was authorized.

Kathy and I count CrossLink International one of the most worthy activities we were ever a part of. We know God led us to Columbia Baptist for a reason. We also know that he put all those professionals together in the same place at the right time to coincide with the unbelievable events taking place in the Soviet Union. CrossLink International was our opportunity and challenge to not just listen to the sermon but put the sermon into action. By our involvement in CrossLink and Prison Fellowship Ministries, I believe our lives have had a God directed purpose. He didn't bring us all the way from Mississippi for nothing. We are so blessed and thankful for all God has done in our lives.

Chapter 32:

RETIREMENT

⊱⊰

On February 1st, 2007 the caravan left the Colson Family Guest House. A moving van, my over-loaded GMC pickup, and our car, packed to the brim, driven by Kathy, headed to Ruckersville, VA. A lite snow was falling, so the short trip took a little longer. We were the third family to move into the promising new community. We had toured the Hovnanian development in Northern VA and were very impressed. We looked forward to our club house getting built and many new neighbors moving in. It was a shock and very depressing when in two years the housing and financial markets collapsed and the economy dived into a severe recession. Hovnanian deserted the development of the community and left town leaving us with a huge Club House designed to accommodate five hundred families. Now the dues of only one hundred and twenty families would have to pay all the expenses for the operation and maintenance of the fabulous club house, the private streets and the open spaces. Our home values dropped overnight. This was not a real concern, for we did not intend to sell. We planned for this to be our final home on this earth.

Our long anticipated, action filled retirement was short lived. We had the devastating news in 2008 that Kathy was having symptoms of dementia. I had noticed some memory problems. Then, one day when she called me from Lee's neighborhood and said she could not find his house, I knew I needed to get her evaluated. We had been to his house many times, and she should have been able to go there. The University of VA Medical Center (UVAMC) did a series of tests that revealed strong dementia issues. Two years later, follow-up tests confirmed that it was the dreaded Alzheimer's. This broke my heart. Kathy was my joy in life. I believe many times I had placed my love of Kathy above my love for God. I was facing a real test of my faith and perseverance.

God always provides in good times as well as bad. Since our retirement in 2007, we have experienced an abundance of wonderful blessings. We have enjoyed our retirement, celebrated and rejoiced in many, many happy occasions, and most importantly we have been surrounded by our boys and their loving families and our church family and friends.

Just as our entire life has been blessed above and beyond anything we could have ever imagined, our retirement years have been blessed even more. When we were busy working and dedicating our time to work and family, the many blessings we experienced were taken for granted and more or less overlooked. Not so with retirement. We now have the time to think about and appreciate every good and perfect gift from our Father. Blessing after blessing started the year of our retirement.

Soon after moving to Ruckersville, we visited two churches near our home. We mentioned to our Daughter-in-Law, Kris, that we were not impressed with the two we had visited. She suggested we try Spring Hill. She had heard good things about it. Fresh out of Seminary, Spring Hill was the first church for Dan Carlton to pastor. He had been there fifteen years, so he must be doing something right. The church was friendly, and we really liked down to earth Dan. Soon after we joined, we discovered they did not have a mixed Sunday School Bible Study for our age group, only a class for men and one for ladies. The part time Assistant Pastor said he would help us get a mixed Small Group started if we would hold a Bible Study in our home. He thought that would be the best way to develop interest in a new Sunday School class. We started the home Bible study with four other couples and two widowers.

One couple was a recently retired pastor, John and Donna Green. They had joined Spring Hill and were also interested in starting a mixed Sunday School class. John and Donna became our very best friends. John led both the new Sunday School Bible Study and the small group home Bible study. He was a scholar of the Bible. I learned much more about the Bible from his teaching than I previously knew. He taught us to appreciate the Bible and how to apply the vast knowledge in it to live our lives in a closer relationship with God. It was a great disappointment when they moved to North Carolina to be near their daughter and granddaughter. But we understood because they also were needed to help care for Donna's mother, who lived to be almost one hundred years old. We are thankful that they come to visit us often.

God has provided untold blessings to us as members of the Christian fellowship at Spring Hill. This beautiful thing called church is providing encouragement, prayer support and Christian fellowship, all of which are helping me cope with the daily challenges of care for Kathy. For over ten years, we have enjoyed an early Saturday morning breakfast with three other Christian couples from church. Our home Bible Study and Sunday School Bible studies have grown and provide prayers and encouragement. Spring Hill is blessed with a new team, Pastor Steve Nethery and wife Ruth. They have been a special blessing by checking on us frequently. I know I face many difficulties, but I am confident that with the prayers and support of my Christian brothers and sisters at

Spring Hill, plus the support and prayers of my family, I can keep my faith and trust in God through these trying times.

This Beautiful Thing Called Church – Spring Hill Baptist Church

Since our retirement, it is unbelievable the joy we have experienced by being able to take trips, attend reunions, celebrate anniversaries, weddings and the birth of another grandson. And now we are very blessed to have both our sons and their families living nearby, providing loving care and support. This is the greatest blessing of all given that we are now in our final years and facing the trials of Alzheimer's. I am very thankful that Kathy seemed to enjoy all of these wonderful occasions. It breaks my heart that she can no longer remember them.

Chapter 33:

ANNIVERSARIES

Kathy and I have always done something special for our wedding anniversaries. For most years it was just a short one or two nights stay some place nearby. This was a time we could recommit and take time out of our busy lives to let one another know how much they are appreciated and loved. For our 40th Anniversary I planned our first real honeymoon. For years I used a Marrriott visa charge card for all our travel credit card charges. The card accumulated points for use at any Marriott Hotel and Resort. Lee had used some of my points for his honeymoon trip to the Caribbean. I arranged our special 40th Anniversary trip well in advance, 4 nights in Oahu and 3 nights in Maui. We would be there the week of October 7th, our anniversary. All our plans were in place at the time of the September 11th terrorist attack. For several days we did not know if the trip would be possible. All flights were grounded, but by October the flights were back to normal. But travelers were not normal. The flight was almost empty. Our hotel was practically empty. They gave us a tour and our choice of any suite we preferred. We chose a beautiful corner room overlooking the Pacific.

My Boarding Pass on September 11, 2001

My personal 9/11 experience was heavy on my heart for a long time. My flight to Atlanta that day could have easily been one the terrorist chose to high-jack. My Delta flight left Dulles International almost exactly the same time the American Flight that returned and crashed into the Pentagon. Near the end of my flight, all of the flight attendants went up to the cockpit. At the time it didn't mean anything. Only later, I realized they had been told what was happening.

The couple in my row were on their honeymoon trip to the Caribbean. I often wondered if they ever got to the Caribbean. As we were landing, I saw there were hundreds of planes on the ground. It still did not register until later that anything was amiss. The pilot did not announce that anything was wrong. Only when we deplaned and walked into the terminal did we realize something had happened.

The terminal was packed, and everyone was standing watching a TV that was showing over and over the planes crashing into the New York World Trade twin towers. I was scheduled to change planes in Atlanta, then travel on to Jackson, MS. My brother, Carey, had flown to Memphis and rented a car the day before and drove to Louisville. We were coming down to be with and celebrate our Dad's 94th birthday on September 13th.

After learning all flights were grounded, and after checking, found there were no rental cars available, I realized I was stranded in Atlanta. There was no reason to stay at the airport, so I rode the metro to downtown Atlanta and decided I would look for a Marriott and check in. I needed to make some phone calls and let everyone know my situation. I found a Marriott and checked in. Atlanta had closed all government offices and sent everyone home because there were rumors that more planes had been hi-jacked. I tried dialing over and over to reach Kathy at work and Carey at my Dad's. I could not get through to anyone. All I got was a busy signal. For nearly three hours, Kathy and her office could not get verification that the flight I was on to Atlanta was not involved. Finally, Lee reached Mom by phone and confirmed it was not my flight that was high-jacked.

After giving up on reaching Kathy or Carey, I called the only person I knew in Atlanta, Ed Miller, my former boss at IBM. I was able to reach him and explain my situation. He insisted that he would pick me up and bring me to his house. So I went down to check out about four hours after I had checked in. I explained why I needed to check out. They didn't charge me for the room. I am sure they were able to fill the room that night. Thousands of people were stranded in Atlanta.

I had vowed I would quit smoking during this trip to Dad's, so I had no cigarettes. Before I checked into the Marriott, I was so in need of a smoke that I had walked all over the hotel in search of a shop that sold cigarettes. Once in the room, I smoked a half pack during the four hours I was there. It would be six more years before I completely stopped smoking.

Finally, in late afternoon I was able to reach Carey at my Dad's. We arranged to meet halfway at Birmingham, AL. Ed had a daughter living in New York at the time and they had not been able to reach her. They were anxious about her situation and did not like to leave the phone in case she tried to reach them. However, about dark we headed for Birmingham in order for me to get to my Dad's in time for his birthday. I was forever grateful to Ed and Barbara for taking me in and driving me to meet up with Carey. Checking with Ed later we learned his daughter was OK. She had also been unable to reach them.

For Dad's birthday, we bought a cake and took him to the Old Roosters club, a group of old men that met at Winston Furniture Store that was owned by Pruitt Calvert, our lifelong friend. The Winston County Journal came up and took Dad's picture with the group celebrating his 94th and published it in the weekly paper. That was a wonderful time for us with Dad. He grew very weak in the next several months. We had to employ help for him in order for him to stay at home. Up to then, he had lived alone after Mom died in 1990. At the age of 96, Dad had a brain aneurysm and died two days later, never having regained consciousness. He died, as he had hoped and prayed, at home without having to suffer.

Our 40th Anniversary trip to Hawaii was a wonderful time. The scenery was beautiful, and the people were very nice and friendly. It was our first real honeymoon. We loved the trip so much that we decided to repeat it for our 45th Anniversary in 2006. The only thing we changed was three nights in Oahu and four nights in Maui. This time the trip was not so great. About half way over I had a severe nose bleed. My right nostril for years would bleed, and Dr. Landes, my ear, nose and throat doctor had cauterized it twice. This time, I guess because of the altitude, we could not get it to stop bleeding. Two Emergency Medical Technicians (EMT's) on our flight finally got the bleeding stopped. EMT's met the flight and took us to a hospital. There they packed it and taped my nose. I could only breath by mouth and my left nostril, which was half blocked because a baseball had hit my nose when I was a boy and I think broke it. I wasn't in pain, but we had to take it easy so I would not get the bleeding started again. We did some guided tours and a luau. It was enjoyable to be in the beautiful place. After returning home, Dr. Landes removed the packing. Thankfully, the bleeding did not start back. Dr. Landes scheduled me for surgery in the hospital. They put me to sleep and he repaired the damaged blood vessel. I am very thankful that the surgery solved my nose bleeding problem, which I had lived with for years.

Our 45th Anniversary trip in 2006 did not end our special anniversary trips. Our next anniversary, found us retired and living in our new home in Ruckersville, VA. We now had no obligations and could be gone as long as we wanted. This time I planned a special anniversary road trip that would take us to several national parks out west. We traveled over six thousand miles. Each day when I determined how far we would go I would call Marriott and reserve a room. We traveled to visit my two nephews, Randy and Jon, Carey's boys. They and their families lived in Plymouth, MN. Their mother, Betty, lived near them. It was wonderful to see them and spend some time where they live. It had been three and a half years since we had seen them. They had come to MS for Dad's funeral in January, 2004.

We then traveled to Fargo, ND. That night in the restaurant where we ate, a group of loud college students were celebrating their sports victory. Two old folks in their mist were very out of place. They were friendly and didn't mind us being there at all. All of our trips have been this way. People all over the United States are friendly and helpful. The next day, we took an automobile tour of Theodore Roosevelt National Park. Not much there other than the Black Hills and the varied terrain. Not much vegetation. Lots of Prairie Dogs.

From there we headed to Montana and the very first National Park, Yellowstone. I planned for us to stay at the Old Faithful Inn on our anniversary night, the 7th of October. Instead of entering the park in the usual entry I wanted to meet up with a couple from our Sunday School class that had moved to Montana. We were meeting them at a restaurant near a not so popular entrance to the park. It was called Bear Mountain Pass. It was a bear. At the end of this narrow, icy, steep, curvy mountain road I was exhausted. My hands were hurting from my having gripped the steering wheel as hard as I could for miles. There were no barriers on the side of this mountain trail. You could not see the bottom of the drop off. Thankfully we only met one vehicle the entire way. It was a road maintenance crew putting salt on the patches of ice. In my opinion the road should not have been open to traffic. I vowed to never travel this type mountain road again. Yet, I went and did the same thing on a mountain road at Rocky Mountain National Park. However, it was wider, had lots of stop offs for grand views and it had barriers, which made a big difference. It was very nerve-wracking to me driving in these vast Rocky Mountains.

When we arrived at Old Faithful Lodge, the parking lot was a quarter of a mile up hill to the lodge. I was suffering from the elevation adjustment and the exhausting trip over Bear Mountain. Our special anniversary dinner that evening was disappointing. I actually felt ill. Our room was decorated with period furniture from the 1800's. No phone, no TV and a not very comfortable bed. I was fine the next morning. Below our room window was a herd of buffalo meandering around.

The highlight of our stay at the Old Faithful Inn was to see Old Faithful in Action. We were scheduled to stay one more night. However, the weather forecast called for blizzard like conditions the next day, so we elected to travel to Billings, Montana and stay two days in a Marriott to ride out the early fall snowstorm. There was a Cracker Barrel nearby, so we relaxed and enjoyed the stay. I worked on the next leg of our trip plans. This was 2007, and even though I was not aware at the time, Kathy was beginning to show signs of dementia. I remember she would repeat her questions that we may have already discussed the day before. She had begun to write down our daily activities, where we went and what we saw. I think she had begun to realize that she could not remember these things. When we were on another long trip in 2009, she wrote constantly and had pages and pages describing our days.

The weather cleared and we left Billings headed for Rapid City, SD. The highway was icy in spots, but we took it slow. The sunshine warmed the highway and it became clear. The Rapid City area was very scenic, and our visit to Mount Rushmore on a beautiful sunny day was a major highlight of our trip. It is a very impressive tribute to four of our greatest Presidents. The history of its creation is a good example of a person dedicated to a cause and willing to see it through against all odds. Also, it was truly brave workers that were willing to risk their lives to accomplish the difficult work that was required.

From Mount Rushmore, we traveled into Colorado to Estes Park where we planned to visit Rocky Mountain National Park, the last park on our schedule. We traveled throughout the park for two days. It is a huge park. Kathy was about to pet a buffalo laying on the ground before I stopped her. Another time a huge moose was in the middle of the road and came very close to our car while we were stopped. Estes Park is a quaint town at the base of Rocky Mountain National Park. Two years later we would have a very rare Livingston Reunion at Estes Park.

Our next trip during retirement was even more rewarding. We would visit six beautiful National Parks. Then we would attend a Livingston reunion at Estes Park, CO. This was the first time we had all been together since Dad's funeral in January 2004. Steve was home from Honduras, so we were blessed to have him travel with us and share the driving. This trip would exceed six thousand miles.

We started the week of July fourth and first visited friends and cousins in Louisville, then on to Kathy's family reunion on the first Saturday after the fourth of July. From there we visited Cousin Dixie and Linda & HO in Pascagoula, MS. Then to Baton Rouge to see our IBM friends, Frank and Jenola Duke. We stayed in Beaumont, TX one night and then to San Antonio to stay two nights with Steve's friend, David Honaker and his wife Mayra. They gave us the grand tour of the city, including the beautiful water walk. Knowing that Kathy was a huge fan of Pioneer biscuit mix because he had eaten them at our house after church breakfasts back in Northern Virginia, David gave us the grand tour of the one and only Pioneer Flour Mill. He treated us to breakfast in the restaurant at the mill. This was an exciting experience to see and know the source of a favorite food item, especially one that Kathy was so fond of and expert in using to make her tasty biscuits. As far as we were concerned, this was a once in a lifetime opportunity.

After San Antonio, we drove and drove across desolate West Texas and almost ran out of gas. We were on fumes and a prayer when we finally made it to civilization. We rushed by scary El Paso hoping we would not need to stop. This was the only city we saw on our entire trip that did not look very nice from the interstate. Our stay that night was in a picturesque locale in Albuquerque, NM. The next day on our way to Flagstaff we saw the Painted Dessert and Petrified Forest. In addition, we took a dessert trail to an Indian village that Kathy's brother, Jerry, had insisted that we visit. It was scary because it was not a tourist village. He insisted we eat at this lone restaurant they operated in their village and have their corn bread. Why we did this I'm not sure. It was a unique experience. This was not a reservation, but an actual Indian community. They did not speak any English and they were not very friendly. We seemed to be the only tourist they had seen in a while. After our disappointing meal at their restaurant, we decided that Jerry had pulled one of his dirty tricks on us by guiding us to this strange, uninviting, way out of the way, non-tourist attraction. We were actually uneasy the entire visit. Jerry never admitted he set us up. He insisted they had really enjoyed the food and the visit to the Indian community.

In Flagstaff we stayed two nights at a hotel on Route 66 and dined at good restaurants in Flagstaff. Each day we made the short trip to Grand Canyon and did a self-guided tour of the many viewing spots. We also enjoyed lunch in the restaurants. Kathy and I had made a quick trip to the Grand Canyon many years ago, after I had attended a training class in Phoenix. It was very exciting for Steve seeing it for the first time.

From Flagstaff, we traveled the back country into Utah for our visit to Zion, Bryce, Canyon Lands and Arches National Parks. We did one day at each and were amazed at the beautiful, awesome and often unbelievable features of God's handy work by nature and weather.

From Utah, we traveled to Estes Park, CO for our Livingston Family Reunion. Lee and his family flew to Denver, then drove a rental car to Estes Park. All the Livingstons had rental houses on the Big Thompson River. One day a small black bear climbed down from one of the giant trees beside Carey and Toni's house. Days were spent hiking and exploring Rocky Mountain National Park. We enjoyed Toni's wonderful cooking for our evening meals. It was a very enjoyable reunion and was probably the last and only time every one of mine and Carey's children and their families will be together on this earth. We are very thankful to God that all our family are believers and serve our Risen Savior.

Our return trip home took us through Kansas City, Saint Louis and Louisville, KY. In Louisville, we had dinner with Steve's friend from Duke, now a professor at The Southern Baptist Theological Seminary.

I am very thankful for the trip. We had learned of Kathy's dementia in 2008. Kathy was writing down daily events, sights, places, time. She was aware that she was not able to remember tomorrow what we did today. Steve and I were overly accommodating in order for her to enjoy every minute of the trip. We would help her with her writing when she would have questions. I am saddened that I didn't finish my memories in time for her to read them, but it is now too late. All of a sudden two years ago she could no longer read. And now when I read to her, she can no longer comprehend the words.

Unlike the trip Kathy and I made to Yellowstone when we got snow bound in Billings, Montana, our six thousand mile trip in the summer of 2009 had perfect weather. I don't recall a drop of rain. A couple of days in Utah it was 110° but the car air conditioner purred right along. On both of our long trips we had no problems of any kind. And I am very thankful that Steve was along for our trip in 2009. Thinking back, if Kathy & I had been alone and something happened to me, I am not sure how Kathy would have been able to do whatever needed to be done. God has always been our co-pilot, including the horrible wreck I caused in 1969. Sometimes He takes us through a bad time to get us to His good plan for us.

Two years later, in 2011, we celebrated our 50th Wedding Anniversary. Kris planned and pulled off a most fantastic celebration. I told her that since our wedding reception was only a small dinner for immediate family at Kathy's Aunt Jewel's home, we wanted to have a great meal and program for all our new church friends and neighbors, plus all the family and friends from out of town that we could get to come. It was a beautiful occasion. We enjoyed a delicious catered meal complete with wedding cake. A photographer was available and provided a picture for each attendee. Kris took care of every detail that you would expect of an expensive reception put on by a professional wedding planner. All of our church friends and some of our neighbors came. Jerry and Bitsy from AL., Carey and Toni from NC, former neighbor

Art and Jewel and their son and his wife came from Northern VA as well as our longtime friend, Mandy Zelaya. Several of Kathy's friends from Prison Fellowship came. My former IBM Manager, Ed Miller from Atlanta came. A very special guest, my nephew, Jon Livingston, from MN came. He had just retired from the Air Force after serving several tours in Iraq.

Thanks to Kris it was a grand celebration. It was held at the lodge at Dover Foxcroft Farm, which is owned by Spring Hill Baptist Church. It has beautiful scenic views of the Blue Ridge Mountains. I cherish this celebration in my memory because at this point Kathy could still enjoy the event and knew everyone's face and name and I think remember the event for some time. I am not sure for how long.

Our 50th Wedding Anniversary Celebration, October, 2011

Chapter 34:

A PRAYER ANSWERED IN GOD'S TIMING

Two years later, 2013, was the year God answered a prayer we had earnestly prayed for over ten years. When Steve first went to Central America as a Missionary, we prayed that he would find a helpmate. We knew we would feel much better if we knew Steve had someone to be with him and help him. We were very much aware that most missionaries went to the foreign field as couples. There were many young ladies from the US that came down to teach in the WGO Ranch school. So I had in mind that maybe God would let this be an opportunity for Steve to meet a good Christian helpmate. This was not to be.

In 2011 while back in the States, Steve received a call regarding one of his boys that had gotten in some trouble at the Ranch. Steve felt led by God to return to Honduras to counsel and assist this young man transition to life on his own in the big city of Tegucigalpa. So he returned for what he considered a temporary task. Steve had known the full time Ranch counselor, Claudia Cecilia Gradiz Canales, for six years while they both worked at the Ranch. However, they had not expressed any interest or feelings for each other. Working together with Cecilia to help this young man, Steve began to consider pursuing a courtship. God was working on answering mine and Kathy's prayers in His own time. On Christmas Eve of 2012, Steve was having the traditional Christmas dinner with Cecilia's parents, and at this dinner he would be asking for permission to have her hand in marriage. On June 20, 2013, Lee, Kathy and I were on a plane bound for Honduras to attend the wedding of Steve and Cecilia on June 22, 2013. We had talked with Cecilia on Facetime, but this would be our first time to meet in person. We had no reservations about her, because we knew Steve's judgment along with God's guidance was enough for us. Anyway, our prayers were finally being answered.

The wedding sight was on top of a mountain overlooking the city. It was perfect wedding weather. The venue had beautiful tropical flowers and wild birds and the elevation provided cool, clean air. The service was packed with over 100 friends and family for Cecilia and Steve. Steve's friends David and Mayra from San Antonio were in the wedding as groomsman and bridesmaid. Steve's pastor from Maryland, Tom Gill, presented the wedding message in English as an interpreter repeated the exact same message in Spanish. This resulted in a longer than normal wedding service, but it was very inspiring.

Steve and Ceci's Beautiful Wedding in Honduras, June 22, 2013

Several of Steve's ranch boys were in attendance. One of the boys took the podium at the reception and addressed Steve as his Dad. This was a great honor to Steve for this young man who had never known his real Dad. It was a beautiful wedding ceremony and outstanding reception meal and program of tributes to Steve and Cecilia. We had wonderful fellowship with Cecilia's mother, father, and brother, Gerardo. Even though there was a language barrier, Steve and Cecilia took care of that. The night prior to the wedding we were invited to the traditional rehearsal dinner at a nice restaurant and were served a traditional Honduran meal. The entire weekend was a joyful time of fellowship for all of us. I was reminded that Christian fellowship is the same everywhere, regardless of nationality. As I said before, I believe the joy of marriages and births are as close to heavenly joy as I think we can experience on earth. This was certainly true when Lee and Steve were married and for the births of their children.

House of Timothy Boys at Steve and Ceci's Wedding

The wedding in Honduras was not enough. We had to have celebrations in the US for their many family and friends to wish them well. Tom and Julie and the church in Maryland did an abbreviated wedding service and had a wonderful catered meal. Every couple was photographed as they arrived, and a picture album was presented to Steve and Cecilia and a copy was given to Kathy and me. All the Maryland church family, Lee and family and Carey and Toni attended. What was amazing, all of Steve's friends from InterVarsity at Duke and their wives attended. They had flown in from various states. They felt obligated, for Steve had been a groomsman or best man in all of their weddings. They each had a prepared speech that entertained us at the embarrassment of Steve. It was revealed they had made a secret pact vowing that all of them would never marry, "Bachelors to the Rapture" or something like that. It turned out Steve was the last holdout. God had other plans for all of them.

We still owed one more group, our church friends and neighbors, the joy of celebrating with us this special occasion. Steve and Cecilia previously had a formal government service which was required for a legal marriage in Honduras. They had the Christian ceremony by Pastor Gill in Honduras and a repeat abbreviated Christian ceremony by the Maryland church family. With all these "I do's," I did not plan another vows ceremony. This would be a celebration reception. Our beautiful new club house had a formal dining room that seated 120. I used the same wonderful caterer that Kris had used for our 50th wedding anniversary. I invited all our Sunday School and small group Bible Study folks plus some additional friends in our Spring Hill church family. I invited several of our neighborhood friends. I invited everyone that I considered special longtime friends, and of course I invited all our immediate family. All total, I invited over ninety, and almost all of them attended. I will not try to name everyone. We had attendees from NC, SC, AL, GA, MS, MN and Northern VA. I introduced Cecilia and Steve, and they gave a little history of how they had come to fall in love. Lee gave a toast for his brother and I gave a short description of their beautiful wedding in Honduras, the pleasure of meeting and getting to know Cecilia's family and the wonderful hospitality we received while there for the wedding. I emphasized how Kathy and I had prayed for Steve to have a helpmate, and after many years our prayers were answered. The delicious meal was enjoyed by all. The invitation requested no gifts; however, many cards were given to Steve and Cecilia and most had checks or cash. I was very pleased with the success of the reception. I had many, many compliments on both the food and the very informal program. I also know the beautiful club house and dining room created an excellent setting for the celebration.

This next event was very special to me. My high school graduation class decided to have a class reunion. It would be fifty five years since the class of 1957 graduated. Louisville High School had seventy two graduates that year. All of us had gone to school together for twelve years. We had a kind of love for each other that only comes from knowing and respecting each other over the years. Our class was really special. Many had successful professional careers. We had no one with even a hint of a criminal record. To me it was a special group of people. The reunion was held at Lake Tiak-O'Khata, the closest thing to a resort in Louisville, MS. We had enjoyable meals and a program the hometown guys had put together. And to top it off, we were entertained by an Elvis Presley impersonator. Elvis was from MS you know, and he was having hit after hit by 1957. I tried to get a reunion going for our 60th but the hometown guys decided it was too much work. It was hinted there may be one more in the future. I hope so, even though I don't think Kathy will be up to it. At the reunion in 2012, Kathy left the hotel room to look for the ice machine. She could not remember the room number. I found her wondering the hall trying to find her way back to the room. From that time on I have always stayed with Kathy and have not left her alone.

Louisville High School Class of 57 Reunion in 2012

Chapter 35:

NEARING THE NEW BEGINNING

⚜

Retirement had nothing to do with the blessing we received in 2015. It was Steve and Cecilia and God's hand of creation. Kathy and I became the proud grandparents for Emanuel Claudio Olen Livingston Gradiz, born May 20th. Cecilia's gynecologist and pediatrician were both late getting to the hospital. Steve, Cecilia and the only on-call doctor at their small hospital delivered little Emanuel. Steve said it was a miracle delivery, as Emanuel was breach and they had already scheduled a caesarean for the 23rd. Of course we were excited and happy for them but it was not easy being so far away and not able to be with them during this special time. It would not be long before we got to hold him. They came for a long visit in July when Emanuel was only two months old. The proud grandparents enjoyed showing off the little bundle of joy. It was really sad when they had to return to Honduras.

At this point Kathy was able to know and comprehend what was happening in the current situation. However, a few minutes or maybe hours, I'm not sure, she would not know what had occurred. She had begun to show agitation and resentment when I was trying to help her with simple tasks. Her frustration was amplified because she could no longer knit. She had used knitting to keep occupied, for she had become unable to cook and do many of the routine duties in the home. I would try to let her do things, but it would end up a big mess and cause her more anxiety. She could still read slowly, watch TV and enjoy music, so we used all those things to stay busy. At this point I typed up the following one page pledge from my heart to let Kathy know I was always trying to help. I would have her read it when she seemed to be upset with me or herself. This written page was the first time she was confronted with the reality of what was happening to us.

May 20th, 2015

Dear Kathy,

Congratulations!! You are a new grandmother. Your new grandson is Emanuel Claudio Olen Livingston Gradiz, Steve and Ceci's new baby. I am writing this down Kathy because your short term memory has stopped working correctly. It is difficult for you to remember. So, I will write down what you and I will need to do from now on. You will need to read this note often everyday so we can both be helpful to each other.

Since your memory is not working correctly, you will need me or someone to get you through each day. I want it to be me and not someone in a nursing home. In order for me to help you, you will need to read this note often and know that whatever I ask you to do it is because I love you and want to help you live here with me rather than somewhere in a facility for Alzheimer's patients.

Please accept this situation and let's make it work as best we can. It will not be easy, but with love for each other and prayers from our family, God will help us. This is not your fault. It is something that many people suffer. We will be an example to others for how well we can work as a team to tackle this terrible disease.

I love you very much. Keith

For over two years she read this many, many times until she could no longer read.

Cecilia's mother passed away shortly after Emanuel was born. She got to see her new grandson. She had battled cancer for a long time. We would like to have been able to be with Steve and Cecilia at this sad time. Our thoughts and prayers were with them and we talked often. Steve set up an internet line where we could talk for free.

Our retirement years became stay at home years as Kathy became less capable. If she had to use a bathroom she might not know to come out and would stay until I sent someone in to help her. One day she slipped away from home. I panicked and had the entire neighborhood searching for her. I called 911, and the police were searching. Low and behold she walked next door to the Orsini's where Joe and Marty were watching a baseball game. She sat there and they did not know that I did not know where she was, so they just let her join them. They both knew she had Alzheimer's but did not know that she did not realize where she was. We were all very happy that she was okay, but Joe and Marty were very embarrassed. Marty apologized to me over and over. I immediately notified the entire community to call me if they see Kathy outside and I am not with her. I now set the security alarm in case I am not aware she has opened the door. The police were very understanding and thought it rather amusing that she was only lost next door.

Kathy and I were no longer taking any overnight trips unless someone was with us. For I knew if anything happened to me she would not be able to cope with the situation. In May 2017, we made an exception and went on an overnight trip to the famous Greenbriar resort in White Sulphur Springs, WV. Our son, Lee, was treating us to an all-expense paid stay at this wonderful resort. He wanted us to be his guest of honor as he was installed as the President of the Virginia Trial Lawyers Association. This was a great accomplishment for Lee. We were so honored and proud for him. He had worked many years for the organization and was very deserving of this recognition. Kris, Annalise and Daniel, Pat and Kathy, Kris's mom and dad, helped make it an enjoyable time for Kathy and myself. Lee's speech was very fitting for the occasion and, more importantly, not too long. The audience of well over two hundred gave him a solid round of applause. The service and food at this resort was the best that I have had the pleasure of enjoying. This was such a proud moment for me. I only wish Kathy could have been able to comprehend how significant this accomplishment was for her son.

Our lives got another wonderful blessing in 2017. Steve and Cecilia notified us that Steve had decided not to continue teaching at the end of school in June. They felt God was leading them to move to the US and Steve would try his hand at his former career, computer programming. They moved into our loft and lived while Steve searched for a job. They wanted to be active in the Maryland church, so Steve was hoping to land a job in Southern Maryland. He had a good interview with a firm but did not hear back. Then his good friend David, best man in his wedding, explained he knew a small firm that needed programmers and he could work from home. This was just the job Steve was praying for. He interviewed and was hired. They located to a nice three-bedroom apartment in an area not far from the Maryland church. They moved in November 2017. We missed them after having them with us over four months and were disappointed they were going to live in Maryland. However, they were only two and a half hours away, which was much, much better than living in Honduras. And we understood their desire to support the Maryland church, for the church had been the financial and prayer support for Steve for many years. During 2018 they came often to visit, and we went to see them several times.

Because of Kathy's continued decline and the burden it placed on me, Steve and Cecilia felt they needed to be closer to us. Since Steve worked from home, they could relocate without it affecting Steve's job. So, at the end of their apartment lease in November 2018, they moved to Ruckersville, VA and would be living only three miles from us. Needless to say, we are very happy to have them and little Emanuel close by.

We are now blessed to have both our boys and their families near us. It is especially comforting to me because if something happens to me, they will be ready to arrange for the care that Kathy needs.

It is love of family that in the end becomes your legacy, and you can bet I am very, very proud of mine and Kathy's legacy.

All the many joys that have been ours, and there have been so very many, were experienced with our church families no matter where we have lived. That is what gave me the idea to name my memories "This Beautiful Thing Called Church." Since I was a boy, the Christian fellowship of believers, called Church, has given my life purpose, guidance, love and support that could not have come from anywhere else. I am truly thankful.

Kathy is no longer really with me, but she knows I am still with her. We are both nearing that new beginning of all joy and no sorrow. This is the blessing of hope for Christians, for we know all about the new Heaven and new Earth which is promised to those that have had their sins erased by the sacrifice of Christ if they believe on Him with their heart and acknowledge Him as their Savior with their mouth.

May God Bless Us All.

CONVERSATION

A Love's Lament by Keith Livingston

Conversations, conversations, have conversations.
Without them all goes away.
Once gone to never return,
for conversation you will forever yearn.

You'll miss the laughter, smiles and cares
that came with those conversations.
Sometimes conversations may bring you tears.
Now the tears may never come to call,
Or tears may flow without a conversation at all.

And now, how can love ever remain and grow
without those conversations we loved before?
Only with conversations in prayer to the One above.
Alas, He will sustain us with His forgiving and gracious love.

CPSIA information can be obtained
at www.ICGtesting.com
Printed in the USA
FSHW011939211019
63226FS